ev+a

2004 – imagine limerick

ev+a 2004 – imagine limerick

published to coincide with ev+a 2004,
Limerick, 13 March – 23 May 2004

ISBN 0946846 197

editorial panel   Paul M O'Reilly
                     Sheila Deegan
                     Mike Fitzpatrick
                     Siobhán O'Reilly
                     Pippa Little

designed + produced for ev+a by Gandon Editions

design   John O'Regan
                (© Gandon Editions, 2004)
production   Nicola Dearey
                Gunther Berkus
photography   Studioworks, Limerick
                (with additional photography by
                the artists)
printing   Nicholson & Bass, Belfast
distribution   Gandon Distribution

GANDON EDITIONS
Oysterhaven, Kinsale, Co Cork, Ireland
tel   +353 (0)21 4770830
fax   +353 (0)21 4770755
e-mail   gandon@eircom.net
web-site   www.gandon-editions.com

Gandon Editions is grant-aided by The Arts Council

ev+a – exhibition of visual+ art

ev+a administration
tel / fax   +353 (0)61 316291
e-mail   evplusartzz@eircom.net
                 info@eva.ie
web-site   www.eva.ie

Limerick City Gallery of Art,
Carnegie Building, Pery Square, Limerick, Ireland
tel   +353 (0)61 310633
fax   +353 (0)61 310228
e-mail   lcgartzz@iol.ie
web-site   www.limerickcity.ie/LCGA

Limerick City Arts Service,
Limerick City Council, Merchant's Quay, Limerick
tel / fax   +353 (0)61 407421
e-mail   artsoff@limerick.ie

cover / pp 2-3   Phil Collins, They Shoot Horses,
                 Ramallah – the first hour
                 2004, DVD video projections, 1 hour
                 (see pages 50-53)

pages 17-18   Anri Sala, Dammi i Colori
                 2003, video projection, 15 1/2 mins
                 (see pages 128-131)

note   dimensions in centimetres
                 – height x width (x depth); video
                 durations in minutes and seconds

note on ev+a – Placing the plus sign (+) inside the name
exhibition of visual+ art, and logo, ev+a, does not represent
the word 'and'. It attempts to call attention to the fact that
the art activity (product and process) engages and
integrates all the senses, not mainly or only the visual
sense. Art springs from how we perceive through all our –
at a recent count – eleven+ senses.

contents

sponsors and patrons — 6
acknowledgements — 8
ev⁺a committee — 8
foreword — 9

essay — imagine limerick — 10
by Zdenka Badovinac

catalogue — ev⁺a 2004 – imagine limerick — 17

open and invited ev⁺a 2004 artists — 18
catalogue (a-z) — 20
map and list of artists by venue — 158

cultural programme of eu presidency
– limerick welcomes slovenia — 160

imagine curating — 162
by Alan Phelan

young ev⁺a 2004 — 172

afterword — points of disorder in the rvm — 180
by Paul M O'Reilly

appendix — ev⁺a story — 185
ev⁺a curators / adjudicators — 186
ev⁺a awards — 187
ev⁺a publications — 188
artists' index — 192

sponsors

corporate patrons

THE ARTS COUNCIL /
    AN CHOMHAIRLE EALAÍON
AIB BETTER IRELAND PROGRAMME
BELLTABLE ARTS CENTRE
BOURN VINCENT GALLERY,
    UNIVERSITY OF LIMERICK
BUS ÉIREANN
CHURCH GALLERY, LIMERICK SCHOOL OF
    ART & DESIGN, and LIT
CLANCY ELECTRICAL
DAGHDHA DANCE COMPANY
DC ELECTRICAL
DEPT OF ARTS, SPORTS & TOURISM
EAGLE STAR
EMBASSY OF AUSTRIA
EMBASSY OF FRANCE
EMBASSY OF MEXICO
EMBASSY OF SLOVENIA
GRANT THORNTON
HALLA ÍDE
IMAGE SUPPLY SYSTEMS
THE IRISH TIMES
KRKA
LIMERICK CHAMBER OF COMMERCE
LIMERICK CITY COUNCIL
LIMERICK CITY GALLERY OF ART
LIMERICK LEADER
LIMERICK YOUTH SERVICE
MODERNA GALERIJA / MUSEUM OF
    MODERN ART, LJUBLJANA
MURRAY O'LAOIRE ARCHITECTS
PHILIPS IRELAND
RTÉ
ST MARY'S CATHEDRAL
SLATTERY'S

CHORUS
CLARK SIGNAGE
CLARION HOTEL
CRAFTPRINT
ITT FLYGT
MICHAEL McNAMARA & CO
O'REILLY HYLAND TIERNEY
MICHAEL PUNCH & PARTNERS
PATTERSON, KEMPSTER & SHORTHALL
BRUCE SHAW PARTNERSHIP
JOHN SISK & SON LTD

Established 1859

Making it possible

EAGLE STAR

EMBASSY OF SLOVENIA

Austrian Embassy
Dublin

Liberté · Égalité · Fraternité
RÉPUBLIQUE FRANÇAISE

EMBASSY OF MEXICO
IN IRELAND

murrayōlaoire
architects

BELLTABLE

LIMERICK INSTITUTE
OF TECHNOLOGY

UNIVERSITY of LIMERICK
OLLSCOIL LUIMNIGH

Department of Arts, Sport and Tourism
AN ROINN EALAÍON, SPÓIRT AGUS TURASÓIREACHTA

www.eu2004.ie

the arts
council
an chomhairle
ealaíon

LIMERICK CITY
GALLERY OF ART

acknowledgements

ACKNOWLEDGEMENTS

All artists, selected and
    unselected, who submitted
    work
Arthur's Quay Shopping Centre
Bourn Vincent Gallery,
    University of Limerick
    – Mary C Sheehan
Damien Brennan
Ger Clancy
Cornerhouse Gallery,
    Manchester
    – Kathy Rae Huffman
Crawford College of Art &
    Design, Cork
Pat Daly
John Deegan
Department of Justice
Oliver Dowling
ESB – Clem Cusack
Executive Travel
Fine Art Services
    – Tony Magennis
Fire Station Artists Studio
Charles Foley
Foras na Gaeilge
Galway Arts Centre
Gandon Editions
    – John O'Regan and
    Nicola Dearey
Maureen Gleeson
Maurice Gunning
Tony Hickey
Image Supply Systems
Catherine Kelly
Noel Kelly
Dan Kenny
Leonard's Garage
Limerick School of Art & Design
    – Bob Baker and Richard
    Ruth, and student
    volunteers: Áine Crowley,
    Simon Dablin, David
    Flanagan, Andrew Forrestal,
    John Galvin, Fiona Goggin,

Celene Natasha Murphy,
    Edith McSweeney
Limerick Senior College student
    volunteers: Hugh Costello,
    Eimear Gavin, Andrew
    Purtill, Eamonn O'Connor,
    Robert Ryan
Limerick Travellers Development
    Group – Margaret Casey
Vincent McCarthy
Étaín MacConghail
Rory McDermott
Richard Meade
Ann Murphy
Máire Ní Ghrada
Helen O'Donnell
Peggy O'Reilly
Michael O'Sullivan
Ormeau Baths Gallery
Mandla Reuter
Gabriel Rosenstock
Sarsfield Bridge Hotel
St Mary's Cathedral
    – Dean Sirr and staff
Shannon Rowing Club
Rev Ger Slattery
Southside Youth Initiative
    – Antoinette McLoughlin
St Mary's Youth Project
    – Jackie Dwane
Sarsfield Bridge Hotel
Studioworks
    – Eamon O'Mahony
3Pcrew – John Gleeson
Jim Tuohy
Brendan Woods
Nives Zalokar
H.E. Mrs Helena Drnovsek
    Zorko, Ambassador of the
    Republic of Slovenia

EV⁺A COMMITTEE

chairman
Hugh Murray

secretary
Sheila Deegan

treasurer
Geraldine Robinson

committee
John Gleeson
Mike Fitzpatrick
Breda Lynch
Helen O'Donnell
Jan O'Sullivan TD
John Shinnors
Roeland von Elsen

administration
Paul M O'Reilly
Limerick City Gallery
of Art
– Mike Fitzpatrick
– Siobhán O'Reilly
– Pippa Little
Limerick City Arts Service
– Sheila Deegan

young ev⁺a administration
– Michael McLoughlin

foreword

The opening of the 28th annual Exhibition of Visual⁺ Art, *Imagine Limerick*, brings forth the selection of Slovenian curator Zdenka Badovinac, who has staged a magnificent exhibition that blends together the work of open submission and invited artists in an engagingly contemporary, conceptually concise, and thematically coherent exhibition. It brings together the work of artists from many countries, and it engages with several significant current social, environmental and political issues. Some of the most interesting artists of our day are included in the exhibition, which makes it a very special experience to enjoy and engage with.

An innovation this year is the further development of young ev⁺a, working with young people in three community groups outside the usual school structures, which has lead to a healthy engagement and interaction with new partners. We particularly welcome the involvement of the AIB Bank Better Ireland Programme in providing generous support for this new direction.

When mentioning our supporters, we must, of course, thank the Arts Council for their continued support of this exhibition, the aim of which is to remain at the forefront of contemporary art practice in Ireland. We also pay particular thanks to Sisk, whose benefit-in-kind support allows us to reach a level of preparation that would otherwise be impossible. We also single out Phillips, who, through Clancy's, provides us with audio-visual equipment. We welcome Eagle Star on board as a new sponsor, and thank each and every local individual and business who provides help in numerous ways to make this a truly citywide engagement with the arts.

Finally, as Limerick is linking with Slovenia as part of the EU enlargement celebrations, and ev⁺a is supported by the cultural programme of of Ireland's presidency of the European Union, we are proud to launch this publication as part of the May 1st celebrations. It is appropriate from ev⁺a's vision and experience to 'Imagine Limerick' as a city that is innovative, experimental and international in outlook.

HUGH MURRAY
chairman of ev⁺a

imagine limerick

I don't recall when exactly I first heard of Limerick – even though it is the third largest city in Ireland – but the name became definitely engraved in my mind when I was invited to curate this year's ev⁺a, Ireland's most extensive international art exhibition. After my initial visit, the preparations for the exhibition required that I travel there a few more times, and every time the journey was a small-scale odyssey. Travelling from one small European city (Ljubljana) to another small European city (Limerick) tends to be more complicated than travelling from one continent to another. Flight connections between small cities are seldom direct, so I usually had to change planes three times. Thus I spent virtually the same amount of time travelling to Limerick as I did staying there, and I used the long hours of waiting about at various airports to conceptualise this project.

I believe art has, in essence, always dealt with some kind of non-belonging, with imagining something that does not exist (yet). The last decade has seen attempts to view all creativity as related to specific socio-political circumstances and to distance it as much as possible from the notion of the autonomy of art and its utopias. The paradox of this situation has always been that the more artists and curators focused on reality and disdained metaphysics of any kind, the quicker they themselves changed their whereabouts and time zones. Curators, who have in some sense dedicated their work to the various relations in space, basically spend most of their time in the non-places of airports (as Marc Augé described places without identity, as opposed to those he called anthropological places, which contain memories of previous places). I would add that non-places are *tabulae rasae* of sorts, places of imagination and expectations, where we imagine – among other things – also the places where we are headed. Non-places are essentially symbols of transformations, places where everyday life changes into a potential adventure, where reality is gradually replaced by fantasy.

I decided long ago that my curatorial approach would not be academic – academic in the sense of some abstract construct I would bring with me to a given referential environment, and there forcefully try to implement it as a framework for my project. Whenever I am invited somewhere as a guest curator I try to base the formulation of my concept on the given situation, on the here and now. But after I had lost so many hours at various airports between Ljubljana and Limerick, this concept of space and time presented itself in a somewhat different light. After my first visit to Limerick I composed a letter for the invited artists in which I related the concepts of real and imaginary spaces. In this relation I found a connection to my own experience of moving from places devoid of memory to an

Gerard Byrne, *Frank and Anne*   2004, live event with video documentation, Limerick City Gallery of Art

environment concerned with the question of (Irish) identity, both in terms of its difficult past and the current issues of globalisation and Europe-isation. This has undoubtedly also influenced my experiencing Limerick as some sort of projection screen where the real constantly transforms into the imaginary, and vice versa. Regardless of how binding reality is, the notions of its possible differentness are no less important than its existence. And to what extent can we separate these two worlds, the real and the artificial one? The new relations between anthropological places and the non-places of the super-modern world can indirectly influence also the revaluation of the relation between the autonomy and the heteronomy of an artwork. In the time of modernism, autonomous artworks represented closed systems, new ideal totalities, utopias that could never be realised. Also, art at the *Imagine Limerick* exhibition imagines new realities, but these are no longer completely new worlds; what is new is essentially only a reorganisation of the already existent. This art does not set out to create an image of an ideal, better world, but is more interested in the infinite possibilities of rearranging matters in its own way.

THE LETTER TO THE ARTISTS

The exhibition *Imagine Limerick*: The aim of the exhibition is to draw attention to the ideology of the visible existence of conflicting interpretations and to the illusory nature of the known. Within the framework of the exhibition, I will try to spotlight the fact that the globalising process gives us the illusion that we actually know the world, whereas general concepts like modernity and tradition do not mean the same everywhere, and, in fact, the interpretation of these concepts can even be quite contradictory in different contexts. The exhibition *Imagine Limerick* will pertain to the relationship between tradition and modernity in Ireland, which can serve, first and foremost, as a model for similar situations all over the world.

Limerick, the host city of ev⁺a, is a small Irish city that is more or less unknown outside Ireland. (Local politicians are trying, among other things, to create a recognisable image for the city in order to attract as many tourists as possible.) In the context of the exhibition *Imagine Limerick*, the name of the city represents something that does not yet have a widely recognised image, and so remains a metaphor for the unknown. Only that which is known, which has an image, exists in the (post)modern world. To have an image is an imperative of the present time. In the broader international context, Limerick still exists somewhere between image and the absence of image, between market and un-market. Limerick shares this fate with most smaller cities that fail to make the list of tourist destinations. And it is precisely for this reason that Limerick, in a world ruled by images, is something special. Everyone who goes to Limerick can freely, without any predetermined images, form his or her own independent idea about it. Limerick stands for all the possible spaces that do not lie in the centre of the world or its communication networks, and which for this reason can become spaces of our imaginations.

It is not expected of participating artists that they should address Irish themes, but rather that they should take the problematic just described more as a model for related issues. Today it is becoming increasingly important to draw attention to how dangerous various forms of generalisation can be and how easy it is for modernisation to become a global process of uniform thinking. For this reason, then, the exhibition *Imagine Limerick* makes a stand for spaces of un-market and imagination.

THE NARROW CONTEXT:
IRELAND BETWEEN TRADITION AND MODERNITY

Centuries of English colonisation have shaped Irish culture, which is marked by both European and post-colonial features. The main theme of Irish cultural studies is the relationship between tradition and modernity. Analysis of this relationship reveals that what is at issue is not a tension between two antitheses, but rather an ambivalent relationship between what are only apparent oppositions. The predominant understanding of modernity is linked to an idea about the linear progress of society, whereas tradition is something that relates to areas of development that have already been traversed. Ireland offers an excellent example of how attempts to explain these notions are always contingent on temporal and spatial contexts. For instance, in many countries with an experience of colonisation, national movements have represented processes of modernisation, although we tend to connect such movements with the notion of tradition, in the sense of non-modernity. For the Irish, liberation from English domination implied a process of modernisation which in art was linked to themes about the endangered Irish tradition.

In present-day discussions, nationality and identity are linked to a reconstruction of history as something that is not clear-cut but, rather, is susceptible to various interpretations. By the same token, these interpretations frequently become tools in the hands of various interests, especially politics and capital, which might, for instance, employ the construction of a traditional ideal image of Ireland in efforts to attract international investment and tourism. The traditional problematic of colonialism has today been replaced by debates about the modernisation of Ireland in the context of liberal capitalist attitudes, which dominate not only the European Union, but global society as well. After Ireland became a member of the EU, the country experienced an economic boom, later developing into the Celtic Tiger, which was greeted with much enthusiasm, especially among advocates of liberal capitalism. On the other hand, however, it was subjected to criticism from various quarters, which stressed how trends toward unification with Europe and global society only made the elite class richer while the problems of social underdogs kept on getting worse.

From the standpoint of conservative circles, however, criticism of modernisation focuses on the move away from tradition, which in this context is understood primarily as nostalgia for harmonious relations between culture, nature and religion. Just like modernity, tradition too appears to be multivalent. The (post)modern reappropriation of tradition can, for instance, be directed towards those elements in Irish society that have an experience of hybridity and multiple identity and are more open towards the Other. Sociologists Michel Peillon and Eamonn Slater, in an attempt to redefine the concepts of tradition and modernity in Ireland, underscore four themes linked to Irish modernity:

1 commodification (characteristic of late modernity and ever more areas of society)
2 globalisation (which leads to the disappearance of the border between Ireland and the rest of the world, as well as giving access to the global flow of signs, images, commodities, exchanges and structures)
3 visualisation (the process by which images and visual symbols become the universal language of commodity production across national boundaries)
4 the aestheticisation of everyday life.

DIFFERENT SELECTIONS

Nowadays it is pointless even to talk about objective selections. In choosing artists for an exhibition, a curator uses many filters, most frequently affected by a certain general taste of the time, and takes few real risks. Great international exhibitions are, as a rule, related to big capital investments, so profit in some form must be guaranteed. For this reason it is the less extensive and seemingly more marginal events that hold more promise of daring and novel ideas.

Compared to the majority of international biennials, ev⁺a displays a special structure. While most exhibitions today adopt similar formulas in the process of selection, which results in the repeated circulation of familiar names that are replaced by new, fresh ones at ever shorter intervals, ev⁺a actually allows for surprises. Its dual principle of selection, with direct invitations to artists (Invited ev⁺a) and a selection of artists who have entered an open international competition (Open ev⁺a), precludes predictable results. I must admit this method of selection also presents a challenge for the curator, since he or she is faced with completely unknown artists.

After I had sent the letter to 22 artists directly inviting them to participate in the *Imagine Limerick* exhibition, I selected another 22 from the five hundred artists who had entered the competition.

THE EXHIBITION

My objective in staging the show was to create as homogeneous a whole as possible, one which would not allow the differences between artists on the grounds of their manner of selection to show. I was only interested in grouping artists in separate theme fields which were all co-ordinated with the general subject of the exhibition reflected in its title, *Imagine Limerick*.

Today, artists seem to operate with the given world, with given forms, materials and situations. At the beginning of the last century, avant-garde artists strove for a fusion with life, often by directly engaging themselves in revolutions, by writing manifestoes, by promulgating new forms of art among the masses through design and architecture. In all this their works often remained, at least apparently, autonomous. Today, artists realise that life itself has become a form, and that therefore the form is no longer only the specific difference which separates art from life, but also a means for art to reintegrate with life – for example, is a picturesque anti-globalisation action that employs a number of symbolic images to a greater extent art or life? The same question applies to an artwork in a gallery space that includes documentary footage or some other form of real life. And is art which speaks directly about a certain political event more political than art which deals with the way images affect reality, a part of which is also politics? In what ways (if any) does it still make sense to separate art from life? Art does more than just capitalise on the power of images (like, for example, politics does); it also demonstrates how they work in a) recognisable and existing reality, b) its abstract signs, and c) matrices from various cultural, social and religious traditions.

In this sense the exhibition is divided into four problem fields. The artists in the *Imagine Realities* section (Carlos Amorales, Yuri Avvakumov & Alyona Kirtsova, Dieter Buchhart, Gerard Byrne, Mircea Cantor, Phil Collins, Mark Cullen & Brian Duggan, Ann Curran, Alexandre da Cunha, Vadim Fishkin, Ben Cain & Tina Gverovic, Eline McGeorge, Emily Jacir, Ilya & Emilia Kabakov, Johanna Kandl, Ziga Kariz, Katrina Maguire, Dorit Margreiter, Maxine Mason, Aisling O'Beirn, Roman Ondak, Vanessa O'Reilly, Anri Sala, Efrat Shvily, Nedko, Veselina & Dimitar Solakov, Apolonija Sustersic, Fiona Tan, Sally Timmons, Aleksandra Vajd) found their place in the Limerick City Gallery of Art and some other venues in the city. These artists include in their works recognisable images of cities, landscapes, well-known objects, portraits, etc, to show what happens to them as they circulate in the media, on the Internet, are transformed into a commodity, or else remain – as part of everyday reality – crucial points of poetic reference, of memory, and of the personal mapping of the world.

The artists in the *Imagine Traditions* section (Maja Bajevic, Sarah Browne, IRWIN, Borut Korosec, Christine Mackey, Paul McAree, Mladen Stilinovic, Anton Vidokle & Julieta Aranda), for the most part exhibiting at the Church Gallery at Limerick School of Art & Design, address the issues of diverse artistic, social and religious traditions, and strive to draw attention to their multifaceted identities, to the possibilities of ideological manipulations and different interpretations generally.

Imagine Signs (Janine Davidson, Ayse Erkmen, Leonora Hennessy, Michael Klien, Volkmar Klien & Ed Lear) is the subject framework of works exhibited in Limerick City Hall and some other venues in the city centre. The contents of works by these artists are related to the various signs used in our communications (the alphabet, city maps and their markings, the sign language of modern technologies), but which are here deprived of their usual functions. Two artists (Alan Phelan, Malin Ståhl) have submitted proposals for projects for this show, which I have classified under *Imagine Curating*. As curators, we tend to try and divide artists' works into some sort of system, either within the concept of a given show or in the sense of classification. This last subject field of *Imagine Limerick* unites all the participants in a different, parallel way, as though there were some 'parasite' curator present, exploiting the existing system merely to prove that the whole thing could have been conceived differently as well.

The exhibition *Imagine Limerick* works with already existing images, signs and systems that we use in our everyday lives to function, communicate, and exert control. The 44 artists transform this existing reality and, with the aid of its elements, imagine different worlds, not because they would necessarily be better than the existing one, but to prove that they are, in fact, possible.

ZDENKA BADOVINAC
curator of *ev⁺a 2004*
Ljubljana, April 2004

Born in Slovenia in 1958. Director of Moderna Galerija / Museum of Modern Art, Ljubljana, since 1993. She has curated numerous exhibitions, presenting both Slovene and international artists.

Her major international projects staged at Moderna Galerija include *Silence – Contradictory Shapes of Truth* (1992); *House in Time* (1995); *The Sense of Order* (1996); *The 1996 Collection*, Museum of Contemporary Art Sarajevo (2000); *Body and the East – from the 1960s to the present* (1998; travelled to Exit Art, New York, in 2001); *2000+ Arteast Collection – The Art of Eastern Europe in Dialogue with the West* (2000; travelled to Orangerie Congress, Innsbruck in 2001, ZKM Karlsruhe in 2002; Umetnicka Galerija Skopje, Cifte Amam, Prostor2, Skopje, in 2002); *Unlimited.nl-3*, DeAppel, Amsterdam (2000); *(un)gemalt*, Sammlung Essl, Kunst der Gegenwart, Klosterneuburg / Vienna (2002; travelled to Moderna Galerija Ljubljana, 2002), *Form Specific* (2003).

Slovene Commissioner at the Venice Biennale (1993-97).
Austrian Commissioner at the São Paulo Biennial (2002).

Board member: IKT, International Association of Curators of Contemporary Art (1999-2002); Comitato scientifico, Museo di Arte Moderna e Contemporanea di Trento e Rovereto (2000); Network 21, Museums Quartier, Vienna (2001); Art Advisory Board, Generali Foundation, Vienna (2001)

Juries: XLVIII Venice Biennale (1999); Central Art Prize of the Central Krankenversicherung an Kölnisher Kunstverein, Cologne (2000); Artist in Residence Program, Atelier Augarten, Vienna (2001); The Vincent 2002, Bonnefantenmuseum, Maastricht (2001); Hiroshima Art Prize, Hiroshima City Museum of Contemporary Art (2001)

She has been invited to participate in many international symposia. She has also published numerous essays and articles on contemporary art.

eva

2004 – imagine limerick

ev+a 2004 artists

Carlos Amorales MEXICO / NETHERLANDS *

Yuri Avvakumov / Alyona Kirtsova RUSSIA *

Maja Bajevic BOSNIA *

Sarah Browne IRELAND

Dieter Buchhart AUSTRIA

Gerard Byrne *

Ben Cain / Tina Gverovic UK / CROATIA

Mircea Cantor ROMANIA / FRANCE *

Phil Collins UK *

Mark Cullen / Brian Duggan IRELAND

Ann Curran IRELAND

Alexandre da Cunha BRAZIL

Janine Davidson IRELAND

Ayse Erkmen TURKEY *

Vadim Fishkin RUSSIA / SLOVENIA *

Leonora Hennessy IRELAND

IRWIN SLOVENIA *

Emily Jacir PALESTINE *

Emilia & Ilya Kabakov RUSSIA / USA *

Johanna Kandl AUSTRIA *

Ziga Kariz SLOVENIA *

Michael Klien AUSTRIA

Volkmar Klien / Ed Lear AUSTRIA / UK

Borut Korosec SLOVENIA

Paul McAree UK

Eline McGeorge NORWAY

Christine Mackey IRELAND

Katrina Maguire IRELAND

Dorit Margreiter AUSTRIA *

Maxine Mason UK

Aisling O'Beirn IRELAND

Roman Ondak SLOVAKIA *

Vanessa O'Reilly IRELAND

Alan Phelan IRELAND

Anri Sala ALBANIA / FRANCE *

Efrat Shvily ISRAEL *

Nedko, Veselina & Dimitar Solakov BULGARIA *

Malin Ståhl SWEDEN

Mladen Stilinovic CROATIA *

Apolonija Sustersic SLOVENIA *

Fiona Tan INDONESIA / NETHERLANDS *

Sally Timmons IRELAND

Aleksandra Vajd SLOVENIA

Anton Vidokle / Julieta Aranda USA / RUSSIA *

* = INVITED ARTIST

18

ev⁺a

2004 – imagine limerick

Carlos Amorales

Born in Mexico in 1970. Studied at Rijksakademie van Beeldende Kunsten, Amsterdam (1996-97). Selected exhibitions: *Nuevos Ricos* (in collaboration with Julian Lede), Chiesa di San Matteo, Associazione Prometeo, Lucca, Italy (2004); *The Nightlife of a Shadow*, Annet Gelink Gallery, Amsterdam (2004); *Stage for an Imaginary Friend*, Galerie Yvon Lambert, Paris (2003); *Amorales vs Amorales, Challenge 2003*, Tate & Egg Live, Tate Modern, London; SF MOMA, San Francisco; Hebbel Theatre, Berlin (2003); *The Bad Sleep Well*, Galerie Yvon Lambert, New York (2003); *We are the World*, Dutch Pavilion, Venice Biennale (2003); *Devil Dance*, Museum Boijmans van Beunigen, Rotterdam (2003); *20 million Mexicans can't be wrong*, South London Gallery (2002). Lives and works in Amsterdam and Mexico City.

The word 'cascara', when translated, literally means 'peel', but in Mexican Spanish it also means the sort of football that people play in the streets – an improvised sort of football match between a few people. In the work *Cascara*, two people play football on a waste ground amongst the rubble left after the demolition of a building. Instead of using an ordinary ball they use a plastic skull.

The way the video is filmed, and the straightforward way it is presented, gives the viewer a very physical sensation, a dizzy feeling, which involves the viewer in the action. With this video I wanted to create an image that, beyond the reality of the action, also functions as a metaphor for the impact all the major political events of the last years have had on me, all the death and destruction. I think the video, because it makes fun of death in a sort of way, is a kind of exorcism. It is a way for me to get rid off all those heavy impressions, the burden they are on me, who lived most of the war events through the filter of the media as a sort of gothic story in which I felt trapped beyond my will.

The video is simple: it has no editing, nor any narrative, but it suggests the action that has happened and is happening in many places in the world. Somewhere soldiers from a foreign army are playing football with the skull of a local old regime; somewhere civilians are playing football with the remains of their own history.

Cascara

2003, one-channel video projection with sound, 15 min loop
venue: Bourn Vincent Gallery, University of Limerick

Yuri Avvakumov / Alyona Kirtsova

YURI AVVAKUMOV was born in Tiraspol, Russia, in 1957, and graduated from Moscow Architecture Institute in 1981. Selected solo exhibitions: *Russian Utopia: A Depository*, Venice, Rotterdam, Moscow, Volgograd, St Petersburg (1996-2000); *1:43*, Karlheinz Meyer Gallery, Karlsruhe (1994); *Temporary Monuments*, State Russian Museum, St Petersburg; State Museum of Architecture, Moscow; *Illiquid Assets*, 1st Gallery, Moscow (1992). ALYONA KIRTSOVA was born in Spitsbergen, Russia, in 1954, and studied painting at Vasily Sitnikov's private school from 1973-75. Selected solo exhibitions: *Retrospection*, Moscow Art Center (2002); *Frankfurt û Aufenthalte*, Galerie im Karmeliterkloster, Frankfurt am Main (1996); *Wine-Green Grass*, Roza Azora Gallery, Moscow (1996); State Russian Museum, St Petersburg (1994).

photography and abstraction, graphics and painting, synthesis and separation, light and colour, image and emotion, Limerick and limericks – memory diptychs

Limerick: 1 – City and county in the southwest of Ireland. 2 – A nonsense poem of five anapaestic lines, of which lines 1, 2, and 5 are of 3 feet and rhyme, and lines 3 and 4 are of 2 feet and rhyme.

Scale: Limerick(s)

2004, ink-jet prints on Arches paper, 76 x 56 cm
(produced with the assistance of ev+a)
venue: Limerick City Gallery of Art

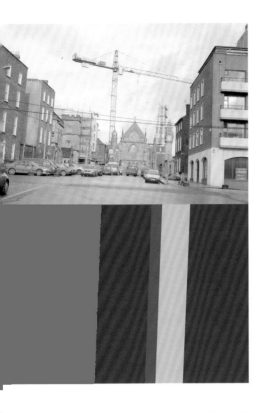

Maja Bajevic

Born in Sarajevo, Bosnia & Herzegovina, in 1967. Education: Diploma Fine Arts, Academy of Sarajevo (1990); MFA, Academy of Sarajevo (1991); Atelier Buraglio, Paris (1996); Ecole Nationale Supérieure des Beaux-Arts, Paris (1997). Selected solo exhibitions and performances: *The Road Movie / Toy of Destiny*, Musée d'Art Moderne de la Ville de Paris (2004); *Psycho*, W139, Amsterdam (2004); *Step by Step*, PS1, New York (2004); *Government*, Kunstraum der Universität Lüneburg (2004); *Good Morning Belgrade*, Museum of Modern Art, Belgrade (2004); *Chambre Avec Vue*, Aussillon (2003); *Plug In*, Basel (2002); *Avanti Popolo*, Viafarini, Milan (2002); *Green, Green Grass of Home*, Artopia, Milan (2002). Selected group exhibitions: 50th Venice Biennale (2003); Turin Biennale (2002); *Manifesta 3*, Ljubljana (2000). Lives and works in Paris and Sarajevo.

There is a noticeable misuse of religion nowadays, which has a whole range of characteristics that separate these new religions, turbo-religions or techno-religions from those that man has been killing in the name of through the centuries. The term turbo-religion signifies for me a form of religion adapted to the comfort of the individual. Through these personalised religions the individual is able to express his difference from the ones not belonging to the same religion, and his connection to the ones belonging to the group. The other part of the game is even worse – nationalism and hatred witch are easily expressed through these turbo-religions. All that in the name of God.

This new way of interpreting religion is not only hurting the religious feeling itself, but is also a sign of deep moral insufficiency and conformism in its worst sense. I am taking different roles from the wide range of new religions, turbo-religions or techno-religions. People feel they have the right to hypocritically reinterpret their religion, and are even proud of it. I want to show the face of nationalism disguised in religion. Contradictions that are usually hidden are coming out. Contradictions that no-one is questioning anymore.

The characters, all of which are played by me, say things like: 'I don't eat pork. I do not drink during the Ramadan. But I take ecstasy.' Or 'I go to church. I rape women.' Putting myself in the role of the interpreter of intellectual and moral rape, I also want to show the displacement one can feel in a world of hidden lies and violence.

Double Bubble
2001, DVD video projection, 3¹/₂ mins
venue: Church Gallery, Limerick School of Art & Design

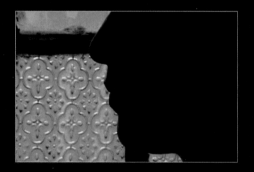

Sarah Browne

Born in Dublin in 1981. Education: BA Fine Art (sculpture), National College of Art & Design, Dublin (1999-2003); Cyprus College of Art (2001); Krakow Academy of Fine Arts, Poland (2002). Exhibitions: Graduate exhibition, NCAD, Dublin (2003); *Green*, Project Arts Centre, Dublin (2003); *Hyperlink*, collaborative web project with Marta Firlet and virtual gallery (www.windaprojekt.com), *Reset*, International Festival of Media Art, Krakow (2002); *The Missing Link*, Guinness Storehouse, Dublin (2001). Lives and works in Co Kildare.

The Gift is conceived of as a participatory artwork involving a handful of particular groups of people and actively engaging with their living space. Six sofas were sourced by the artist, re-covered with a particular pattern, and distributed as gifts to people who might not otherwise be consumers of gallery-based art. The printed pattern, constructed from Irish White Potatoes packaging and iconic text from the Declaration of Independence, addresses notions of lifestyle and identity, and how such ideas are linked to physical and cultural consumption. The pattern exists as the artist's intervention on an old, disused piece of furniture, giving it new life and conferring upon it a potential new value.

The sofa is given in exchange for documentation of the object in its new environment, using such lens-based processes as video and photography, and is completely negotiable with the participant. Money is bypassed in these transactions. These are exchanges based on something else – transactions of trust – and must be undertaken with a genuine and respectful spirit on both sides. The timeframe for the video lasts only as long as appropriate: it is important not to overstay a welcome, and when the tea is drunk, the video camera is turned off and it is time to go. The sofas exist as tokens for sparking an interaction between people, and are not sold, but distributed as gifts. Their worth does not lie in their exchange value, but in their capacity to be used in an ordinary living space, to catalyse a dialogue with an alternative audience. It is hoped that the representation of these sofas in such an environment will serve to open up a mental space outside that of the gallery/exhibition space.

The Gift

2003, mixed media installation with sofas, video, book and display materials, dimensions variable
venue: Church Gallery, Limerick School of Art & Design

35

Dieter Buchhart

Born in Vienna in 1971. Studied biology and art history at the University of Vienna. Since the early 1990s he has been working in public space, landscapes and indoors, integrating friends, acquaintances, visitors and passers-by in his artworks. Solo exhibitions: Institute for Contemporary Art, Copenhagen (2004); *Museum in Progress*, Vienna (2000); Simultanhalle, Cologne (2000). Group exhibitions include: Museum für Kunst & Gewerbe, Hamburg (2004); *Crawford Open 4*, Crawford Gallery, Cork (2003); Nikolaj Contemporary Art Center (Copenhagen, 2002); Austrian Gallery Belvedere, Vienna (2002). Lives and works in Vienna.

how to build a house
when someone loses everything he or she sometimes tries to build a new house.
to destroy a house is much easier than to build one.
building a house is sometimes as cold as owning no house.
speed sometimes kills while building a house.
building a house is like having much fun.
it is a pity that not everybody can afford to build a house.
taking a break while building a house might be dangerous.
building a house is like having sex under a bridge.
building a house means taking much responsibility for society.
building a house might also mean to take much responsibility for yourself.
building a house is a great chance.
society needs you to build a house.
loosing your house is like being on the street without a house.
house unknown
building site unknown
construction worker unknown
architect unknown
city does it matter?
building a house is like being anonymous.
music (recorded during filming)
dieter buchhart 1998-2001

how to build a house
1998-2001, DVD video
venue: Chamber of Commerce

Gerard Byrne

Born in Dublin in 1969. Selected solo exhibitions: BAK, Utrecht, The Netherlands (2004); Frankfurter Kunstverein, Frankfurt (2003); Douglas Hyde Gallery, Dublin (2002); Limerick City Gallery of Art (2001). Selected group exhibitions: *This Much is Certain*, Royal College of Art, London (2004); Institution @ Kiasma, Helsinki (2003); Istanbul Biennale (2003); *The American Effect*, Whitney Museum of American Art, New York (2003); *Stop & Go*, FRAC, Pas-de-Calais (2003); *Greyscale / CMYK*, Tramway, Glasgow (2002); *Manifesta 4*, Portikus, Frankfurt (2002); *How Things Turn Out*, Irish Museum of Modern Art, Dublin (2002).

A conversation at the opening of *ev+a 2004* between some other conversations. The conversation will be overheard by everyone, one person at a time. The conversation will be intimate, and at the same time generic. A film of sorts, without a camera.

The scenario involves two actors playing a couple. The actors will 'attend' the opening as regular visitors. They will, however, be miked, using radio microphones. Their conversation will be relayed using the mics to a receiver, where it will be monitored, recorded (as documentation), and, most importantly, relayed back to the crowd via a single set of radio headphones. The radio headphones will be passed among the crowd by a helper, as a sort of conspicuous communal pass-around. The actors will not use a script, but will improvise a conversation based on a number of ideas/parameters I will give them.

The conversation will take cues from a number of films: for example, the basic scenario – a couple walking and conversing in a crowded space – from *The Conversation* (Coppola); an aural schism between the lone headphone-wearing listener and the surrounding crowd – *Wings of Desire* (Wenders); and the citation of seemingly arbitrary objects from the spatial situation as an improvised script – the notice board in the final scene of *The Usual Suspects*.

A video camera will record the crowd from the balcony of the City Art Gallery. The camera will pick out faces, and seemingly search the crowd for the source of the conversation, without ever actually locating the specific couple. Subsequently, the conversation will be edited together with the footage of the crowd. The subsequent video material will be screened as a document of the event for the duration of the exhibition.

Frank and Anne
2004, live event with video documentation
(produced with the assistance of ev+a)
venue: Limerick City Gallery of Art

While the herd naturally assumes spatial formations based on internal hierarchical principles, they would also appear to respond to the 'presence' of spectators. As the position of the camera was moved, so too did the herd reconfigure positions in response to the camera's changed position. The photographs were taken from a relatively close range of approximately twelve metres. At this range the herd assumed a studied nonchalance, which seemed strangely anthropomorphic, almost learned. Nevertheless, individual deer would take up specific positions in relation to both other individuals and to the changing camera position, whilst others would remain static. Once the new configuration was assumed, the deer would resume relatively static stances. As a whole, the herd appeared to maintain a carefully unified, choreographed façade to the camera that speaks of some self-awareness of the herd's collective 'appearance' as a spectacle.

The direct descendants of the Duke of Ormond's deer herd, maintained in the Phoenix Park, Dublin, since the 1650s
2003, photographic sequence, each 63.5 x 53.5 cm
(courtesy Green on Red Gallery, Dublin)
venue: Limerick City Gallery of Art

Ben Cain / Tina Gverovic

TINA GVEROVIC was born in Zagreb in 1975. Graduated Academy of Fine Arts, Zagreb (1997); Jan van Eyck Akademie, Maastricht (2002). Lives and works in Zagreb. BEN CAIN was born in Leeds in 1975. Education: Foundation Studies, Leeds College of Art & Design (1993-94); BA Interactive Arts, Manchester Metropolitan University (1994-97); MA, Jan van Eyck Akademie, Maastricht (1998-2000). Lives and works in Zagreb, Leeds, London. Selected joint exhibitions: *Third Part*, Gliptoteka, Zagreb (2004); *After the City*, Modern Art Gallery, Split, Croatia (2003); *Film You*, Mediator, Dubrovnik, Croatia (2002)l *Untitled*, Fordham Gallery, London (2001); *Room 4*, Belgrade Cultural Centre (2001); *Lectures on Lectures*, Halle für Kunst, Lunaberg (2000). As well as collaborating on artworks, both artists also work and exhibit independently.

The work planned for Limerick looks at the influences of imagination, given stereotypes and memory on documentary and on creating ideas and visions of a place. In this case, addressing the viewer's position means thinking about how subjects in art, and how visions and ideas of a place can be created by a viewer quite subjectively and individually. In this case, the physical reality and present time of the gallery space is placed beside seemingly fictional accounts of another time and place. There would be two spaces generated: the here and now of the gallery space, which is theatrical and stage-like, and the elsewhere of ideas and images associated with another place that is suggested by sound. Together these two spaces play with subjects related to physical and immaterial, real and virtual. The work might also question the role that geographical information, as well as information of names and dates, plays in describing place. It might also raise questions about the influence that language and voice has on the perception of place and history.

Visitors and the Modern City

2004, mixed-media installation, dimensions variable
(produced with the assistance of ev⁺a)
venue: Limerick City Gallery of Art

Mircea Cantor

Born in Transylvania, Romania, in 1977. Co-editor of *Version* magazine (www.versionmagazine.com). Solo exhibitions: *Corporate Identity*, FRAC des Pays de la Loire, Carquefou (2003); Galerie Yvon Lambert, Paris (2003); *In front of my eyes*, Trans Area, New York (2003); *The Right Man at the Right Place*, Galerie Yvon Lambert, Paris (2002); *Nulle part ailleurs*, Le Studio Yvon Lambert, Paris (2002); *Ping Pang Pong*, Entre-deux Association, Nantes (2002). Selected group exhibitions: *Quicksand*, DeAppel, Amsterdam (2004); *The Happy Worker*, Bard College, Anandale-on-Hudson, NY (2004); *New Video, New Europe*, Renaissance Society, Chicago (2004); *In the Gorges of the Balkans*, Kunsthalle Fridericianum, Kassel (2003); *Displaced*, UCLA Hammer Museum, Los Angeles (2003); 50th Venice Biennale (2003). Currently living and working in Paris.

Under the guise of an ordinary street demonstration, The Landscape is Changing *inverts one of the essential characteristics of this type of protest. Whereas normally the multiplication of individual enthusiasm creates an autonomous and powerful collective energy, the demonstrators in* The Landscape is Changing *seem to release an individual energy which escapes and surpasses them. Crossing this urban theatre, where the weight of the architecture symbolises a political omnipresence, the cortège simply opposes its inoffensive mirrors to the seats of power they pass by, thus reinforcing their indifference to the immediate context. The variety of shooting angles and the perfect organisation of the march strengthens the unity of the cortège, which rapidly takes the shape of a moving 'thought'. In a traditional demonstration, the agitation and cries of the crowd allow a group release of personal feelings. On the contrary, Mircea Cantor's calm and silent cortège concentrates itself on the singular vision of the artist. Thus, the collective question mark is gradually transformed into a personal question mark.*

— Amiel Grumberg
(from catalogue essay for *Quicksand*, DeAppel, Amsterdam)

The Landscape is Changing
2003, video projection, 22 mins
(courtesy Mircea Cantor and Yvon Lambert, Paris /
New York)
venue: Limerick City Gallery of Art

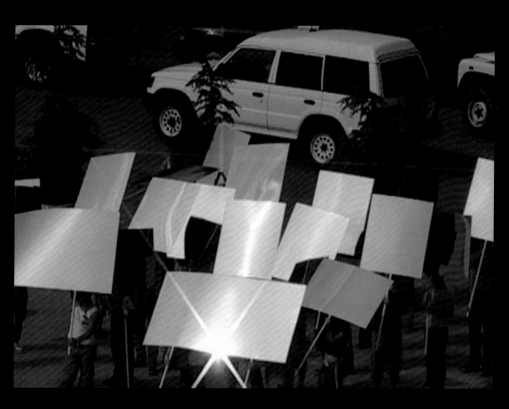

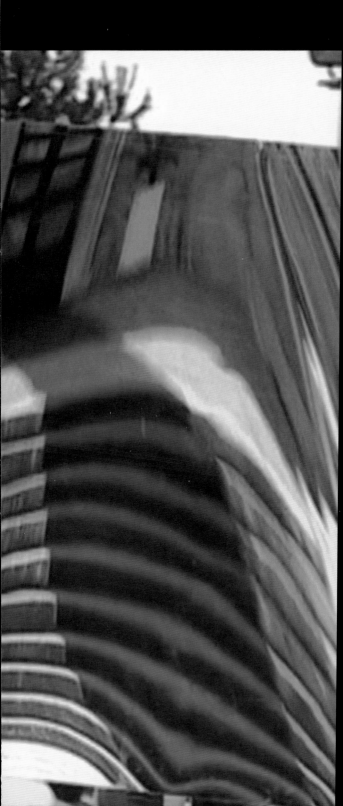

Phil Collins

Born in Runcorn, UK, in 1970. Studied at University of Ulster, Belfast. Selected solo exhibitions: Maccarone Inc, New York (2003); *Real Society*, Ormeau Baths Gallery, Belfast (2003); *Baghdad Screen Tests*, Meeting House Square, Dublin (2003); *Bad Infinity 2*, Locust Projects, Miami (2002); *Becoming More Like Us*, Artopia, Milan, and Temple Bar Gallery, Dublin (2002); *Reproduction. Time Wasted.*, London Print Studio (2002); Kappatos Gallery, Athens (2002); *Bad Infinity*, Kerlin Gallery, Dublin (2002); *Mislim ne Znam*, Meeting House Square, Dublin (2002); *Face Value*, Context Gallery, Derry (2001). Selected group exhibitions; *Present Futures*, Turin (2003); *Now What? Dreaming a Better World in Six Parts*, BAK, Utrecht (2003); *Art Now Lightbox*, Tate Britain, London (2003); *Reality Check*, British Council touring show (2002). Lives and works in Brighton.

They Shoot Horses is an eight-hour disco dance marathon filmed in February 2004 in Ramallah. The work was produced by ev⁺a, Al-Mamal Foundation, Kerlin Gallery, and the Popular Art Centre, Ramallah.

They Shoot Horses, Ramallah – the first hour

2004, DVD video projections, 1 hour

(co-commissioned by ev⁺a and the Al-Mamal Foundation, Jerusalem; thanks to the British Council)

venue: Halla Íde, Thomas Street

Mark Cullen / Brian Duggan

MARK CULLEN and BRIAN DUGGAN work separately and together on numerous artistic projects, exhibiting regularly. In 1996 they created Pallas Studios, which emerged as a leading representative of innovative art and cultural projects in Ireland. Pallas was established to engage, harness and provoke the independent art landscape (www.pallasstudios.org). They have recently developed Pallas Heights – alternative exhibition spaces in a semi-derelict housing block in Dublin's inner city. They live and work in Dublin.

In November 2003 Mark Cullen and Brian Duggan set up a new mixed group in Donomore / Killinarden, in west Tallaght, Dublin. This project, orientated towards the youth of the area, made several original short digital films over nine months. The group, who were all 16 years old, had no experience in film-making. The films are the result of weekly workshops, discussions and arguments, ideas, notes, dreams and throw-away comments. During the process the new group visited some of Dublin's most prestigious galleries – the Hugh Lane Gallery, the Irish Museum of Modern Art, the RHA and the Douglas Hyde – for the first time. They found the work there interesting, but in general the response to the video work on display was 'not impressed, we could do better'. The project is called *Short Shorts*. During this project eight short digital films were made:

Killinarden Killers – A horror genre tale of break-and-entry into the local school. *LFS (Local Fitness Survival)* – This film takes stereotypes associated with housing sprawl and turns them on their head in a comic satire involving a host of the community. *The Gulf War II* – Using news footage and local interviews, this documentary investigates our responses to the war. *Still Time* – This is a series of portraits and landscape tableaus animated and put to a score, to give a sense of a day in the life of any suburban estate. *Dinner in a Glass* – An urban take with the gender issues surrounding food and eating. *The Spike* – A cautionary tale of young social interaction, that gets out of control with sinister implications. *Soft Scrutiny* – An ode from the individual, in the social spaghetti junction that is the modern shopping centre. *Devil Car* – The goings-on in the hills of Killinarden.

Short Shorts

2003, eight digital films
(the artists worked with Edel Cummins, Michael Usher, Denise Gaines, Lorraine Smith, Wesley Brennan and Terence Salmon. *Short Shorts* was funded by the South Dublin Co Council as part of a Percent for Art project.)

venues: films being shown in various city centre locations

Ann Curran

Born in Dublin. Received an MA from the Visual Studies Workshop, Rochester, New York. Has exhibited in both the US and Ireland. Currently lecturer in photography at the Burren College of Art, Co Clare, and lives in both Ballyvaughan and Dublin.

On 12 January 2003 I made a journey across nine time zones from Vienna, Austria, to Los Angeles, California. From 7am to 4pm I travelled from live web-camera to web-camera, over mountains and roadways and cities, capturing one image from each camera as I went along, heading west. The web-cameras I visited were put in place for seemingly benign and pleasurable purposes – to show weather conditions or provide views of cities or winter resorts for prospective tourists. Placed on the highest peaks, they invoke the eye of God looking down from above and surveillance on a vast scale. This grid of views is a representation of space and time across a vast physical distance on a particular day. It is a composite portrait of a winter landscape across two continents, and a document of a journey taken and not taken.

My work is an exploration of locations, imagined or real. Ultimately the image becomes a memory or stand-in for the experience of being there, and it is that process of substitution that I am most interested in. People move around these days; relocation is a common thing. Time becomes stretched and condensed to suit our needs. Mapping out a space, a location, or a set of places is a process of mediation. Even when the images supplied by memory are true to life, one can place little confidence in them.

Vertigo
2003, ink-jet prints on watercolour paper, linen tape,
wooden dowels, brass hooks, grid: 4.9 x 1.8 m
venue: Limerick City Gallery of Art

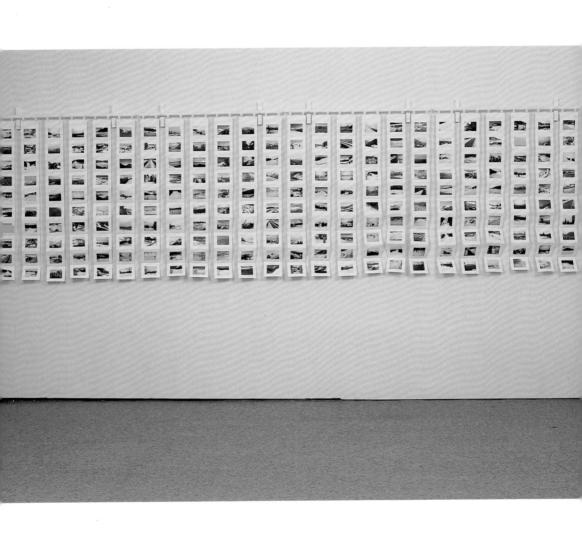

Alexandre da Cunha

Born in Rio de Janeiro, Brazil, in 1969. Selected
exhibitions: 50th Venice Biennale (2003); *The Virgin
Show*, Wrong Gallery, New York (2003); *The Lost
Collection of an Invisible Man*, Laing Art Gallery,
Newcastle (2003); *PoT*, Liverpool Biennial (2002);
Alexandre da Cunha + Brian Griffiths, Galeria Luisa
Strina, São Paulo (2002); *PICAF*, Pusan
International Contemporary Art Festival, Pusan,
Korea (2000); *ev·a 2000 friends + neighbours*,
Limerick City Gallery of Art (2000); *Herancas
Contemporaneas*, MAC, São Paulo (1999); *Projeto
Macunaima*, Funarte, Rio de Janeiro (1998);
European Media Art Festival, Osnabrück, Germany
(1997). Lives and works in London.

Fans

2003, found skateboards, metal bowls and
metal components, 113 x 120 x 113 cm
venue: Limerick City Gallery of Art

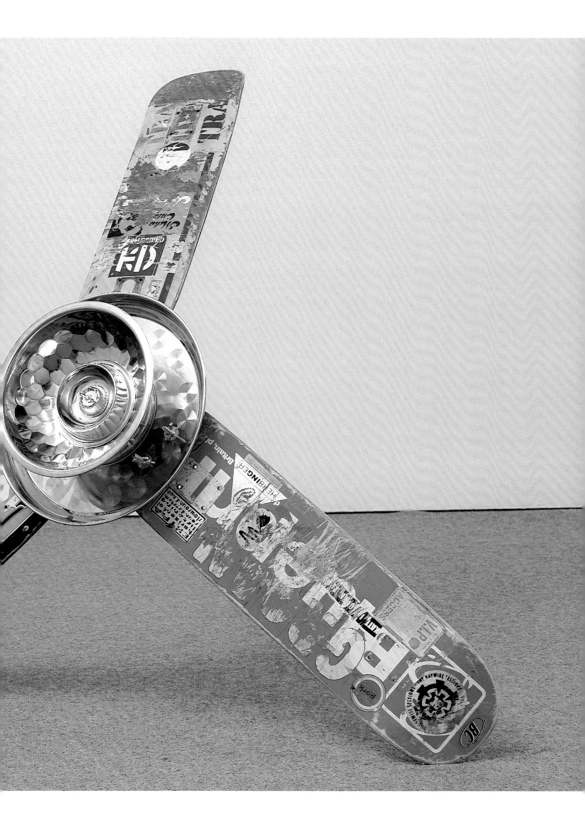

Janine Davidson

Born in 1974. Education: BA Fine Art (printmaking), National College of Art & Design, Dublin (1993-97); postgraduate in community arts, NCAD (2002-03). Residencies at Artist's Proof Studios, Johannesburg (2003-04). Exhibitions: *50/50*, Temple Bar Gallery, Dublin (2003); Christmas Show, Belfast Print Workshop (2003); National Arts Club, New York (2003); *Prints from the Blackchurch*, Courthouse Arts Centre, Tinahely, Co Wicklow (2003); *About Us*, Artist's Proof Gallery, Johannesburg (2003); *20/20*, Temple Bar Gallery, Dublin (2002); *Grafiska Sallskapet*, Stockholm (2002); *Metamorphosis*, Original Print Gallery,Dublin (2002); *Impressions 8/2002*,Galway Arts Centre (2002); *Íontas 2000, 11th National Small Works Exhibition*, Sligo Art Gallery; Ormeau Baths Gallery, Belfast; Limerick City Gallery of Art (2000). Lives and works in Dublin.

This piece is part of an ongoing body of work in response to my residency in Johannesburg, South Africa. South Africa has not yet fully emerged from the shadows of violence. As a result, Johannesburg is a very challenging city to negotiate. These pieces refer to the huge car culture inherent in South African society. They deal with themes of navigation and repeated journeys. The tactile and often delicate nature of the work represents the fragility of existence in Johannesburg. Embroidery is also a major element of South African culture, both as a craft used to create income and as a means of recording stories of people and the past.

This particular piece has great resonance for my personal practice as it was first conceived at the Artist's Proof Studios, which was devastated by a fire. Tragically, a fellow artist, Nhlanlha Xaba, died in the blaze. The main impetus behind my work is to create an accessible visual language that reflects societal and cultural concerns.

Via Via
2003, embossed hahnemuhle paper with gold thread, dimensions variable
venue: City Hall, Merchant's Quay

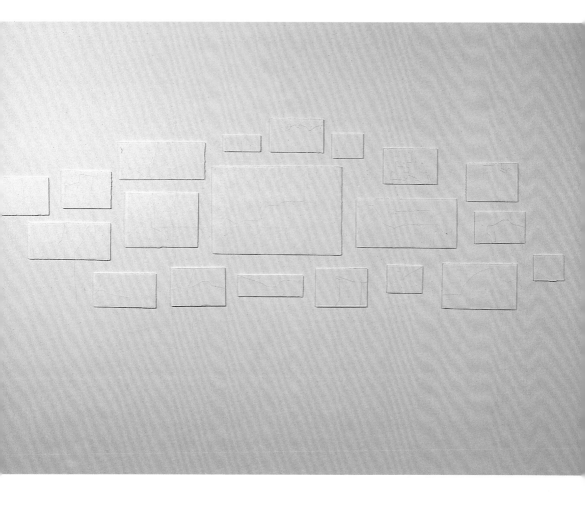

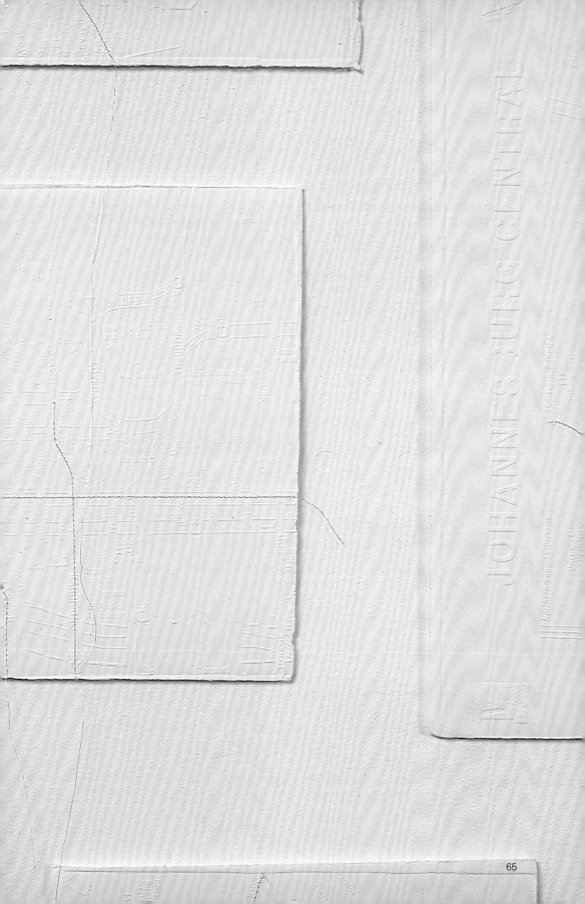

Ayse Erkmen

Born in Turkey. Selected solo exhibitions: *Kuckuck*, Kunstmuseum St Gallen, Switzerland (2003); *Tidvatten*, Magazin 3, Stockholm (2003); *Kein gutes Zeichen*, Secession, Vienna (2002); *Ketty & Assam*, Kokerei Zollverein, Essen (2002); *Müßiggang*, Galerie Barbara Weiss, Berlin (2002); *Bos Zamanlar*, Galerist, Istanbul (2002); *Shipped Ships*, Frankfurt am Main (2001); *Half of*, Galerie Deux, Tokyo (2000). Selected group exhibitions: *Material-Immaterial*, Kunsthalle Mannheim (2004); *Who is singing over there?*, National Gallery of Bosnia & Herzegovina (2004); *Performative Installations*, Galerie im Tazisplais, Innsbruck (2003); *Niemand ist eine Insel*, Gessellschaft für Aktuelle Kunst, Bremen (2003); Berlin Biennial (2001); *Looking At You*, Museum Fridericianum, Kassel (2001); Kwanju Biennial, Korea (2000). Lives and works in Germany.

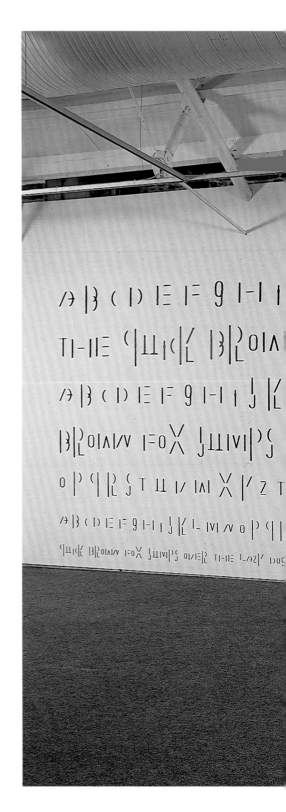

Untitled

2004, adhesive vinyl, dimensions variable
(produced with the assistance of ev⁺a)
venue: City Hall

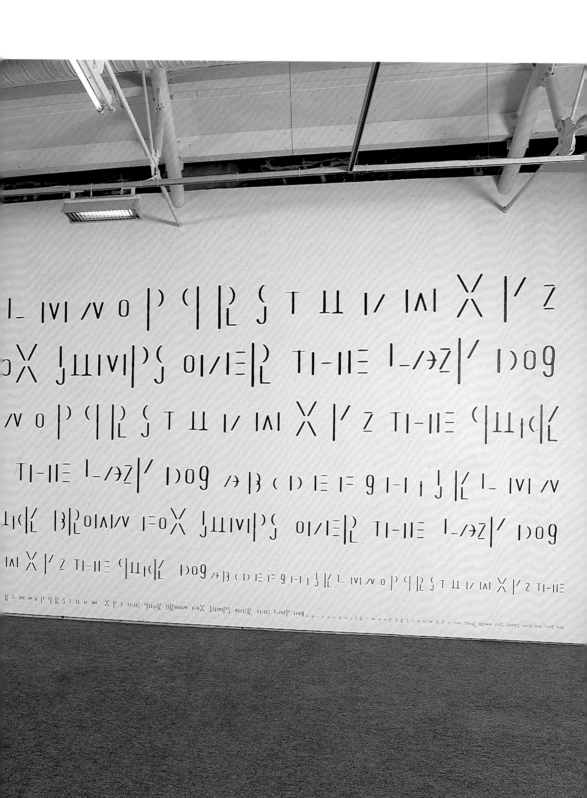

Vadim Fishkin

Born in Penza, USSR, in 1965. Graduated from Moscow Institute of Architecture in 1986. Selected solo exhibitions: *Dictionary of Imaginary Places*, Galerija Skuc, Ljubljana (2002); *Snow Show*, TV Gallery, Moscow (2000); *Dedicated*, Gallery Knoll, Vienna (1998); Isabella Stewart Gardner Museum, Boston (1997); *Reason is Something*, Venice Biennale (1995); Mala Galerija, Ljubljana Museum of Modern Art (1995). Selected group exhibitions: *Free Entrance*, BAWAG Foundation, Vienna (2004); *Imagining Prometheus*, Palazzo della Ragione, Milan (2003); *Station Utopia*, Venice Biennale (2003); *Berlin-Moscow / Moscow-Berlin*, Martin Gropius Bau, Berlin (2003); *MIR: Art in Variable Gravity*, Cornerhouse Gallery, Manchester (2003); *Iconoclash*, ZKM, Center for Art and Media, Karlsruhe (2002). Lives and works in Ljubljana and Moscow.

In a review of The Dictionary of Imaginary Places, *a book to which Vadim Fishkin's work of the same name refers, it says that* 'The Dictionary of Imaginary Places *is best described as a guidebook of the make-believe'. Fishkin's* Dictionary *is both a poetic variation on the make-believe and a carefully added place of imagination, which the artist has wrung out of the book. On a screen the visitor sees rhythmic frequency waves produced by two different voices: one distorted and deep, the other high-pitched and rather nervous. They recite the names of places and countries, all of them strangely shrouded in mystery and some of them familiar to us from the history of literature.'*

— Gregor Podnar
from *Vulgata*, 3rd Triennale of Contemporary Slovene Art, Museum of Modern Art, Ljubljana, 2000

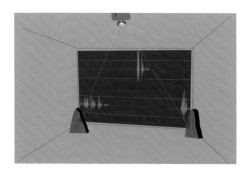

Dictionary of Imaginary Places
2000-04, computer-generated projection, stereo sound, 2 loudspeakers, red light, dimensions variable, 54 min loop
(producer: Association DUM, Ljubljana)
venue: Limerick City Gallery of Art

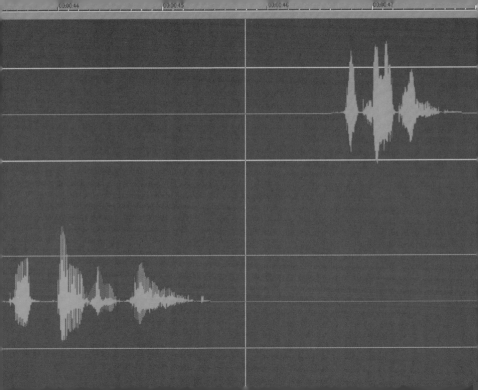

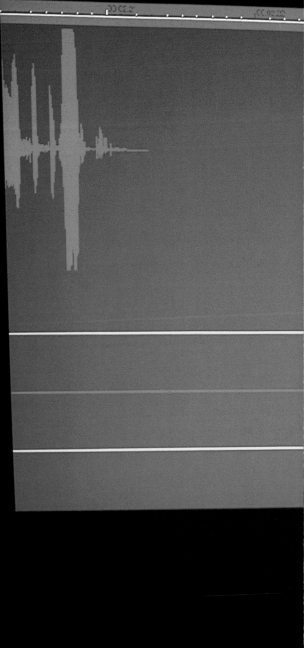

Leonora Hennessy

Education: BA in Fine Art, Limerick School of Art & Design (1999); MFA, Glasgow School of Art (2003); Skowhegan School of Painting & Sculpture, USA (2002). Selected exhibitions (2004 / 2003): Galeria Central del Centro Nacional de las Artes, Mexico City; *Homemade*, Kunstlerhaus Mousonturm, Frankfurt; *De Een Minuten*, The Netherlands; *Accommodation 2*, Edinburgh; Portobello Film Festival, London; *Tent*, Rotterdam; Groundswell Foundation Benefit, White Columns, New York; *Rock Candy*, Hotel Mariakapel, Hoorn, The Netherlands; *How to undo Spells with String*, Intermedia, Glasgow. Selected awards: Hope-Scott Trust (2002); Skowhegan Fellowship (2002); Limerick County Council Arts Bursary (2001).

Some motivations and strategies when considering space:

Negating a sense of dislocation
Creating a sense of location
Locating myself
Building a space
Tag an existing space
Denying a space
Placing and curating objects
Confronting a space
Using space to house my own hope, humour and failure

These and other strategies help my attempts to make bold statements out of the ordinary, insignificant or forgotten. My work to date has encompassed painting, sculpture, sound, video, installation and web-based projects. In this somewhat disparate practice, investigations into drawing and space act as a common denominator. Much of my work originates from investigations into a sense of place and how it is intrinsic to, or even formed by our relationships with the object world.

As I continue to redefine the parameters of drawing within my practice, this work endeavours to question the use of line to describe space in both real and illusory terms.

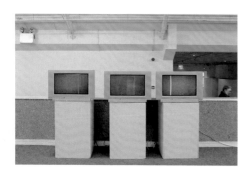

Untitled (TV Line)
2003, DVD video
venue: City Hall

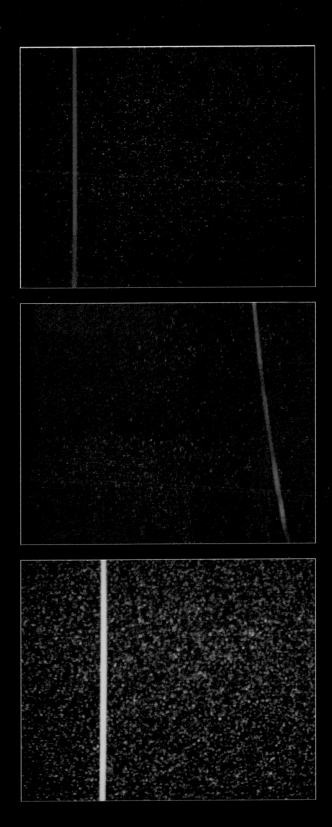

73

IRWIN

IRWIN was founded in 1983. It consists of DUSAN MANDI (born in Ljubljana in 1954), MIRAN MOHAR (born in Novo Mesto, Slovenia, in 1958), ANDREJ SAVSKI (born in Ljubljana in 1961), ROMAN URANJEK (born in Trbovlje, Slovenia, in 1961), and BORUT VOGELNIK (born in Kranj, Slovenia, in 1959). Selected exhibitions include: Cornerhouse Gallery, Manchester (2004); Museum of Modern Art, Belgrade (2004); Kunstlerhaus Bethanien, Berlin (2003); Galerie Inge Baecker, Cologne (2003); Galerija SKUC, Ljubljana (2003); *Rekapitulacija*, Museum Ostdeutsche Galerie, Regensburg, Germany (2002); *New Works*, Galerie Grita Insam, Vienna (2001); *Retroavantgarde*, Galeria Bonomo, Bari, and Obala Art Center, Sarajevo (2001); *IRWIN Live*, Museum of Modern Art, Ljubljana (2000).

Like to Like consists of photographs documenting apparent artistic interventions in the landscape. These are, in fact, re-stagings of the activities of the1960s and 70s Slovene conceptual group OHO, the only remaining evidence of which is meticulous plans and grainy black and white photos. IRWIN's piece augments this documentation with bigger colour images, giving the happenings an apparent clarity and weight.

Like to Like
2003-04, colour photographs
(thanks to Kathy Rae Huffman, Director, Cornerhouse Gallery, Manchester)
venue: Church Gallery, Limerick School of Art & Design

Like to Like / water-air

2004, photo reconstruction of the OHO (Marko Poganik)
action *Family of fire, air and water: water-air* from 1969
(photos: Toma Gregori; courtesy Cornerhouse Gallery, Manchester)

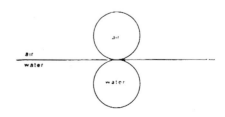

Like to Like / The constellation of candles in the field
corresponding to the constellation of the stars in the sky
2004, photo reconstruction of the OHO (Milenko Matanovi) action
The constellation of candles in the field corresponding to the
constellation of the stars in the sky from 1970.

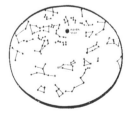

Emily Jacir

Solo exhibitions include: Khalil Sakakini Cultural Centre, Ramallah, Palestine (forthcoming); Nuova Icona, Venice (forthcoming); *Debs & Co*, New York and O-K Center for Contemporary Art, Linz, Austria (2003). Has participated in numerous group exhibitions, including the 8th International Istanbul Biennial (2003); MOMA, Oxford; Apex Art, New York; La Panaderia, Mexico City; PS1 Contemporary Art Center, New York; Queens Museum of Art, New York, and will be included in the 2004 biennial at the Whitney Museum of American Art, New York. Lives and works in Ramallah and New York.

Austrian nationals Marwan Abado, Peter Rosmanith and Franz Hautzinger were invited to perform on July 25th, 2003, in Jerusalem, and July 26th in Bethlehem as part of the 12th Jerusalem Festival *Songs of Freedom* concert series organised by Yabous Productions.

Abado, who is of Palestinian origin, was officially invited by the Austrian Embassy in Tel Aviv, as well as the United Nations Development Programme. He obtained a visa through the Israeli Foreign Ministry in Vienna prior to his arrival. On July 20th, 2002, Marwan Abado arrived at Tel Aviv's Ben Gurion airport and was immediately detained by the Israeli authorities. After being held for 24 hours in the airport prison (a representative from the Austrian Embassy, who had come to welcome him, remained with him during this time), Israeli security cancelled his visa and he was put on the next plane back to Vienna. He was denied entry into Israel for 'security reasons'. No further explanation was given.

Marwan is one of hundreds from around the world – filmmakers, artists, doctors, lawyers, students, government officials, human rights workers, etc – who has been refused entry by Israeli security, with the official reason given being 'security'. They are targeted because they are working with or helping Palestinians.

I asked Marwan and his band to imagine that they were in Jerusalem and to perform the concert.

Entry Denied (a concert in Jerusalem)
2003, DVD video projection with poster, 105 mins
(thanks to O-K Center for Contemporary Art, Linz, Austria
for both production and photo)
venue: Limerick City Gallery of Art

مهرجان القدس — أناشيد الحرية
JERUSALEM Festival Songs of Freedom

Left program

مهرجان القدس
أناشيد الحرية

Festival
Songs of Freedom

20 - 29 / 7 / 2003

20-7 أمسية الافتتاح
أوج
جوقة الغناء العربي في المعهد الوطني للموسيقى
Awj Arabic Choral Ensemble of NCM
Palestine فلسطين

21-7 زِمـار
Zimar
Palestine فلسطين

22-7 رباعي إريك تروفاز
Erik Truffaz Quartet
France فرنسا

23-7 لوارنا لوبر
Luar Na Lubre
Spain اسبانيا

24-7 سيبونجيل كومالو
Sibongile Khumalo
South Africa جنوب افريقيا

25-7 مسك وعنبر
Misk wa Anbar
Palestine/Austria فلسطين/النمسا

26-7 ريم بنا
Rim Banna
Palestine فلسطين

27-7 بلاك اومفولوسي
Black Umfolosi
Zimbabwe زمبابوي

28-7 كلابيون
Quilapayun
Chile تشيلي

29-7 أمسية الاختتام
فرقة الموسيقى الشرقية
Oriental Music Ensemble NCM
المعهد الوطني للموسيقى
Palestine فلسطين

Tombs of the Kings, Jerusalem, at 8:00 pm
تقام جميع العروض في قبور السلاطين الساعة الثامنة مساء

بالتعاون مع القنصلية الفرنسية العامة في القدس
In cooperation with Consulate General of France - Jerusalem

عروض بيت لحم بالتنسيق مع دار الندوة الدولية
المعهد الوطني للموسيقى
Bethlehem performances are in cooperation with
The International Center of Bethlehem - National Conservatory of Music

yabous
productions
للإنتاج الفني

Right — Tickets Prices

أسعار التذاكر
Tickets Prices

Adult	35
Student, over 60, Disabled	25
Child (under 6)	15
Family (2 adults, 2 children under 15 years old)	70
Golden Ticket for all concerts	200

Official Hotels of the Festival:
Jerusalem:
Christmas Hotel
Ambassador Hotel
Az-Zahra Hotel
7 Arches Hotel
Capitol Hotel
Jerusalem Hotel
Meridian Hotel
Bethlehem:
Santa Maria Hotel

Official Restaurants:
Jerusalem:
Sizzling
Askidinya
Pasha's of Jerusalem
Eldorado Internet/Café
Az-Zahra (Az-Zahra Hotel)
Al-Taboon (Christmas Hotel)
Lotus & Olive Garden (Jerusalem Meridian Hotel)
La Bistro (7 Arches Hotel)
Antonios & Addiwan (Ambassador Hotel)
KanZaman (Jerusalem Hotel)
Ramallah:
Angelo's
Kanbata Zaman
Sangria's
Stones
Haifa:
Fattoush

- Tickets will be sold at Yabous Productions' information desk at the Christmas Hotel - Jerusalem, starting from the 10th of July 2003, during the hours 10.30 - 12.30, and 15:00 - 18:00.
- Daily sale of tickets during the festival will take place at the St. George's Schoolyard - Jerusalem starting at 19:00.
- Car parking facilities are available at the St. Georges School, Nablus road - Jerusalem, near Tombs of the Kings.
- Student's identification cards are requested for discount.
- Special discount offers for groups of min. 10 persons from clubs, organizations and institutions valid until 15th of July 2003.
- 10% discount given by the official hotels of the festival, on accommodation rates to audience of the festival upon presenting the ticket of that day's concert or the golden ticket.
- 10% discount given by the official restaurants of the festival, for meals or drinks to audience of the festival upon presenting the ticket of the (same day's concert or the golden ticket.
- 10% discount on all products of "Siniora/Al Quds" (Al-Haya Food Industries Co.Ltd.) provided upon presenting the festival's ticket or newspapers advertisements.

يقام المهرجان بدعم من:

الاتحاد الأوروبي - سيدا / وكالة التنمية الدولية السويدية - القنصلية الاسبانية العامة ومكتب التعاونية الاسباني - برنامج الأمم المتحدة الإنمائي - مكتب تمثيل جنوب افريقيا - شركة الحياة للصناعات الغذائية ذ.م.م. - مؤسسة فورد - جوال / الشبكة الفلسطينية الأولى - الحكومة البلجيكية - ع. الياس رض. للبناء والتطوير - مؤسسة عبد المحسن القطان - البعثة البابوية لفلسطين - بلدية فيينا - TV5

The Jerusalem Festival is funded by
European Union - Sida/Swedish International Development Agency - Consulate General of Spain / Spanish Cooperation Office - UNDP/United Nations Development Program/Tokten program - South African Representative Office - Al-Haya Food Industries Co. Ltd. - Ford Foundation - JAWWAL The First Palestinian Network - Belgian Government - A.M. Qattan Foundation - Pontifical Mission for Palestine - Elias Akkawi Ltd for construction and development - Vienna Municipality-TV5

For more information and reservations please contact Yabous Productions, Tel: (02) 6261045, e-mail: randa@yabous.org
حجز ولمزيد من المعلومات الرجاء الاتصال بمؤسسة يبوس للإنتاج الفني، هاتف: 6261045 (02) - بريد الكتروني randa@yabous.org

79

Emilia & Ilya Kabakov

Selected solo exhibitions: *The Empty Museum*, Sculpture Center, Long Island City (2004); *20 ways to get an Apple, and other works by Ilya & Emilia Kabakov*, Sean Kelly Gallery, New York (2004); stage installation for *St François d'Assise*, opera by Olivier Messiah, Ruhr Triennale, Bochum, Germany (2003); *Not everyone will be taken into the future*, permanent installation, MAK Museum, Vienna (2002); *The Palace of Projects*, permanent installation, Kokerci Foundation, Essen (2001); Retrospective, Kunstmuseum, Bern (1999). Have participated in numerous group exhibitions, including Documenta, Kassel; Whitney Biennial, New York; Venice Biennale. Live and work in the USA.

An enormous table occupies a disproportionate space in the room; only a narrow space is left for the viewer to get around the table, by flattening himself against the wall. The table is covered with a white tablecloth, and plates and silverware are arranged in rows of place settings. A drawing lies to the left of each setting, and a text to the right. In the middle of the table is an apple, placed in such a way that it is impossible to reach it from any side of the table. The room is draped in white fabric. The music of Mozart can be heard in the room. The drawings and texts on the table should be examined by the viewer moving clockwise around the table. The text explains a 'way' to get the apple. For each of the twenty place settings, this 'way' is new and unexpected. Together the ways represent a large 'fan' of possibilities: philosophical, linguistic, magical, technological, psychological, political, etc. Each way is described in extraordinary detail, and in a sense this represents a small encyclopedia of all possible ways of appropriation, except, of course, the simplest and least accessible way – to grab it. The drawings serve as a visual commentary on the texts. All of this has an extremely grave and profound appearance, but the atmosphere of the installation – the white walls, the white curtains, the lighting and the music – imparts to the whole a nuance of playfulness, festivity, and irony.

(text adapted from I & E Kabakov, *Monument to a Lost Civilisation* (Milan, 1999))

The twenty ways to get an apple listening to the music of Mozart
installation, dimensions variable, site-specific (courtesy Moderna Galerija, Ljubljana)
venue: Limerick City Gallery of Art

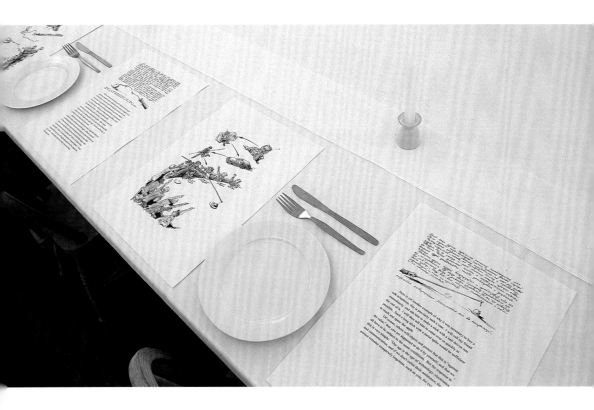

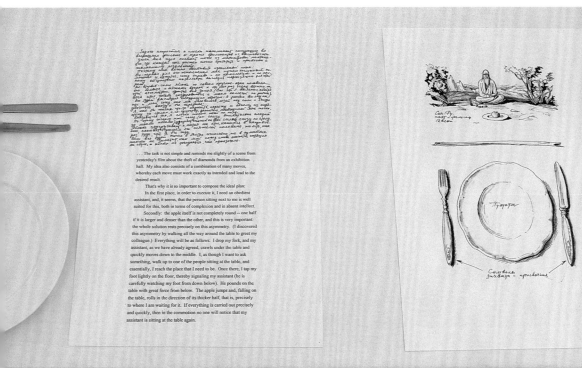

. . . The task is not simple and reminds me slightly of a scene from
yesterday's film about the theft of diamonds from an exhibition
hall. My idea also consists of a combination of many moves,
whereby each move must work exactly as intended and lead to the
desired result.

That's why it is so important to compose the ideal plan:

In the first place, in order to execute it, I need an obedient
assistant, and, it seems, that the person sitting next to me is well
suited for this, both in terms of complexion and in absent intellect.

Secondly: the apple itself is not completely round — one half
if it is larger and denser than the other, and this is very important:
the whole solution rests precisely on this asymmetry. (I discovered
this asymmetry by walking all the way around the table to greet my
colleague.) Everything will be as follows: I drop my fork, and my
assistant, as we have already agreed, crawls under the table and
quickly moves down to the middle. I, as though I want to ask
something, walk up to one of the people sitting at the table, and
essentially, I reach the place that I need to be. Once there, I tap my
foot lightly on the floor, thereby signaling my assistant (he is
carefully watching my foot from down below). He pounds on the
table with great force from below. The apple jumps and, falling on
the table, rolls in the direction of its thicker half, that is, precisely
to where I am waiting for it. If everything is carried out precisely
and quickly, then in the commotion no one will notice that my
assistant is sitting at the table again.

Johanna Kandl

Studied painting in Vienna and Belgrade. Selected solo exhibitions: *Nobody knows what will happen next*, Galerie Friedrich / Ungar, Munich (2004); 9th Cairo Biennale (2003); Kunstverein Ulm (2003); Galerie Christine König, Vienna (2002); Galerie für Zeitgenssische Kunst, Leipzig (2002); Secession, Vienna (1999). Selected group exhibitions: *Identitt Schreiben*, Galerie für Zeitgenssische Kunst, Leipzig (2003); Werkleitz Biennale (with Helmut Kandl), Germany (2002); *Painting on the Move*, Kunsthalle, Basel (2002); *Uncommon Denominator*, MassMOCA, North Adams, USA (2002). Lives and works in Berlin and Vienna.

The Cleansing of the Temple
2004, temporary street drawing
venue: Cruise's Street

Ziga Kariz

Born in Ljubljana, Slovenia, in 1973. Selected solo exhibitions: *Terror=Decor: Art Now*, 50th Venice Biennale, Slovenian Pavilion, Venice (2003); *Movie Tales* (in collaboration with Tobias Putrih), Skuc Gallery, Ljubljana (2001); *Terror=Decor II: High – Concept*, Mala Galerija, Museum of Modern Art, Ljubljana (2000). Selected group exhibitions: *Media in Painting*, Cankarjev dom Gallery, Ljubljana (2004); *U3*, 4th Triennial of Contemporary Slovene Art, Museum of Modern Art, Ljubljana (2003); *Toxic*, Max Protetch Gallery, NY (2003); *Iconography of Metropolis*, São Paulo Biennale, Brazil (2002); *Gravity Zero*, Uppsala Konstmuseum, Sweden (2001). Lives and works in Ljubljana.

Televisual image, with its telepresence of spectacular images, is the theme of the paintings by Ziga Kariz; there, the screen is the means of beaming the images of urban catastrophe and violence, among others, into the private sphere. Kariz makes the iconosphere of televisual and film violence confront the artistic language and elements of modernism, mostly derived from the work of Piet Mondrian. The juxtaposition of contemporary visual escalation of the images of fear with the asceticism of modernist utopia of form that regulates social interaction proves to be a far-reaching commentary on post-modernist preoccupation with mirror images, reflecting ideological conflict and the spectacle function of the media. The Kariz picture is all at once an investigation of contemporaneity, such as it is seen in media images, and a reflection of previous artistic definitions of form, as seen in, and transformed by, contemporary events. This confronting of the avant-garde utopia with the spectacle of violence thus ends up in a sophisticated insight into the genealogy of contemporaneity, where the avant-garde utopia acquires the function of quality design, with the world of images escalating into previously unimagined forms.

— Tomislav Vignjeviz
(from catalogue essay for *Media in Painting*, Cankarjev dom Gallery)

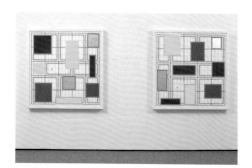

Terror=Decor: Art Now 3
2003, wall-painting and mixed-media objects,
139 x 139 x 12.5 cm
venue: Limerick City Gallery of Art

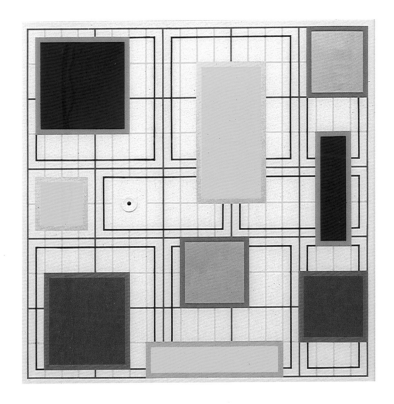

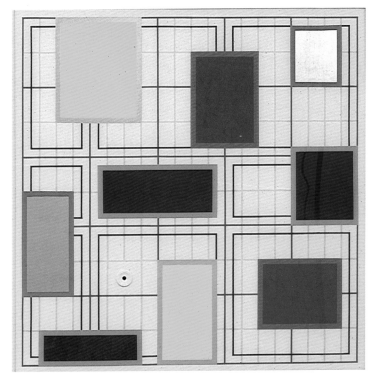

Michael Klien

MICHAEL KLIEN was born in Hollabrunn, near Vienna, in 1973. Currently artistic director of Daghdha Dance Company in Limerick. Artistic co-director of London-based arts group Barriedale Operahouse from 1994-2000. His work as a choreographer, director and producer has been shown throughout Europe, and includes commissions for Ballett Frankfurt, ICA, ZKM and Volksoper Wien. Currently working on a PhD at Nottingham Trent University. Curator of *SHIFTS*, contemporary choreography, culture and technology event (1999-2000). Winner of the Bonnie Bird Choreography Award in 1998. Further information: www.michaelklien.com.
NICK ROTHWELL (programmer) has done programming work for a number of arts-related projects, including Ballett Frankfurt and Volksoper Wien. Further information: www.cassiel.com.

A sentimental entity on a patch of green grass. If the world doesn't revolve around it at least it wobbles in its direction occasionally. A working mind spread across the fields of the social, the ordinary and the in-between. The lamp is equipped with the capabilities to gain knowledge, to build meaning and to express itself in a limited manner. It gathers information in Slattery's pub and uses its light to communicate its findings. To fully perceive and engage with Slattery's lamp is an exercise in trust.

Slattery's lamp – sediments of a mind
2004, light installation, 3.5m x 80cm x 30cm
(produced with the assistance of ev+a, and supported by Daghdha Dance Company)
venue: Slattery's

93

Volkmar Klien / Ed Lear

ED LEAR was born in England in 1971. Completed a degree in Visual Arts & Music at Oxford Brookes University. Currently studying for a PhD in Electroacoustic Composition at City University, London. Recent exhibitions include Dartington Arts & Contemporary Music, Oxford, with commissions for new work from Helsinki and Taipei. Lives and works in Devon, England. VOLKMAR KLIEN was born in Hollabrunn, near Vienna, in 1971, where he later studied philosophy and composition. Also received a PhD from City University, London. Lecturer at the University for Music & Performing Arts in Vienna since 2002. Most recent presentations of his work include concerts and installations at festivals and institutions, including ZKM, Ballet Frankfurt, Volksoper Wien, ICA London, and Huddersfield Festival of Contemporary Music.

Everything starts with a pub tour. Couple of drinks, couple of cigarettes, off to the next bar. Couple of drinks, couple of cigarettes. Then – moving on. Next day, same thing. Couple of drinks with a couple of cigarettes in a couple of pubs.

In each of the pubs we leave behind a nice silvery lighter. Each silvery lighter equipped with a nice little transmitter and its own transmission ID.

And above the roofs antennas rise.

The next couple of weeks we spend roaming the urban habitat, tracking the lighters, tracing the fire, logging its every move.

Traces of Fire
2004, mixed-media documentation of a city-wide tracking project
(produced with the assistance of ev⁺a, and supported by the Austrian Embassy)

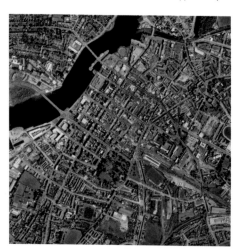 

...er No.1: Planted March 15th 2004 at 'Slattery's' on Lord Edward Street
Transmission Frequency: 150.005 MHz

...er No.2: Planted March 16th 2004 at 'The Square Bar' on John's Square
Transmission Frequency: 150.105 MHz

...er No.3: Planted March 16th 2004 at 'The Launch' on St. John's Street
Transmission Frequency: 150.155 MHz

Planted March 15th 2004 at the 'White House' on Glentworth Str.
Transmission Frequency: 150.205 MHz

Planted March 15th 2004 at the 'Wolf Tone Bar' on Wolfe Tone Street
Transmission Frequency: 150.255 MHz

...er No.6: Planted March 16th 2004 at 'Holy Ground' on St. John's Str.
Transmission Frequency: 150.305 MHz

...er No.7: Planted March 16th 2004 at the 'Wolf Tone Bar' on Wolfe Tone Str.
Transmission Frequency: 150.355 MHz

...er No.8: Planted March 16th 2004 at 'Nancy Blake's' on Upper Denmark Str.
Transmission Frequency: 150.405 MHz

...er No.9: Planted March 16th 2004 at 'Portley's' on Lock Quay
Transmission Frequency: 150.455 MHz

...er No.10: Planted March 15th 2004 at 'South's' on Quinlan Street
Transmission Frequency: 150.505 MHz

Borut Korosec

Born in Ljubljana, Slovenia, in 1968. Studied sculpture at the Academy of Fine Arts, Ljubljana, graduating in 1997. Selected recent exhibitions: *Visura Aperta*, multimedia festival, Momjan, Croatia (2003); *Girls from Biennial*, Start, Zagreb, Croatia (2003); *Metropolitan Iconographies*, São Paulo Biennial, Brazil (2002); *Poetry of the Winds*, Flag Art Festival, Seoul, South Korea (2002); *Kitchen* (with P Seliskar), Celjski Likovni Salon, Celje, Slovenia (2002); *Great Orton*, Galerija Alkatraz, Ljubljana (2001). 'With my work I am questioning my positions, from which it could be possible to add something to the world.' Lives and works in Ljubljana.

Future matters, because we are there already. Considering that I am now writing a text that you will get in a few minutes and give to others to be used as part of a catalogue, which will then be printed in the following weeks and possibly be read by someone unknown in the even more distant future... It can be understood that these lines can be seen as a seed and not as a fruit. I can imagine that an experience of the world (or of an art exhibition, if you wish) takes the same orientation towards future, because we are all there already.

Commandments

2003, computer with video projection
venue: Church Gallery, Limerick School of Art & Design

soundglass

u shall have no other gods before Me.You shall not make for yourself a carved image—any likeness of anything that is
aven above, or that is in the earth beneath, or that is in the water under the earth.You shall not take the name of the L
ur God in vain.Remember the Sabbath day, to keep it holy.Honor your father and your mother.You shall not murder.Yo
all not commit adultery.You shall not steal.You shall not bear false witness against your neighbor.You shall not covet yo
ighbor's house.You shall not covet your neighbor's wife.

pocketmoney

You shall have no other gods before Me.You shall not make for yourself a carved image—any likeness of anything that is
eaven above, or that is in the earth beneath, or that is in the water under the earth.You shall not take the name of the L
our God in vain.Remember the Sabbath day, to keep it holy.Honor your father and your mother.You shall not murder.Y
hall not commit adultery.You shall not steal.You shall not bear false witness against your neighbor.You shall not covet y
neighbor's house.You shall not covet your neighbor's wife.

have no other gods before Me. You shall not make for yourself a carved image—any likeness of anything that is in heaven above, or that is in the earth beneath, or that is in the water under the earth
the name of the LORD your God in vain. Remember the Sabbath day, to keep it holy. Honor your father and your mother. You shall not murder. You shall not commit adultery. You shall not steal. You sh
ess against your neighbor. You shall not covet your neighbor's house. You shall not covet your neighbor's wife.

Paul McAree

Born in Cork in 1972. Education: BA Fine Art, Limerick (1991-95); MA Fine Art, Birmingham, UK (1996-97). Exhibitions: *Offer it all up* (in collaboration with Mona Casey), Birmingham (2003); *Nth Art 00*, London (2003); *Lux Open 2003*, Royal College of Art, London; National Gallery of Ireland, Dublin (2003); Göethe Institute, Dublin (2003); *Tabula Rasa*, various outdoor sites, Croydon, London (2002), Liverpool Biennial (in collaboration with Mona Casey), Liverpool (2002); *Appropriation*, Ormeau Baths Gallery, Belfast (2002). Lives and works in London.

West is an installation of paintings looking at the reconstruction and recycling of Irish history and its cultural representations. The installation refers to post-independence Ireland's attempt to create an art that captured the soul of Ireland, where the west of Ireland became the most significant theme in nationalist aspirations. This vision of the west was harnessed by the State, and artists like Paul Henry and Jack B Yeats created a new Irish iconography in the form of the heroic peasant and landscape.

The work positions the nationalistic struggle for cultural identity (via representations of sea, mountains and certain historical political images) within a more global framework. The sea paintings are based upon Henry's *Launching the Curragh*, while the mountains are based on typical representations of the west of Ireland by Henry, Jack B Yeats and Seán Keating.

The role of the photograph/source image is reduced to that of a source and catalyst for a broader discussion on painting. Historical images are sieved, and through repeated painting individual meanings become diffused into a collective interpretation. The paintings acknowledge that the construction of meaning is social, institutional and contestable in its positioning of Irish culture in relation to western art. The aim here is to discover not what each painting may refer to, but how their juxtaposition may constitute meaning.

West

2004, painting and mixed media installation, dimensions variable
venue: Church Gallery, Limerick School of Art & Design

Eline McGeorge

Born in Norway in 1970. Education: Oslo University (1990-92); Oslo Drawing and Painting School (1992-94); Staatliche Hochschule für Bildende Künste, Frankfurt am Main (1997); Vestlandets Kunstakademi, Bergen, Norway (1994-98); MFA, Goldsmith's College, London (1998-2000). Recent group exhibitions: Butler Gallery, Kilkenny (2004); *Transmogrifications*, Danielle Arnaud, London (2004); *Unexpected Elsewhere*, Gallery Niklas von Bartha, London (2003); *Break in Theatre*, Hara Museum, Tokyo (2003); *ev·a 2003*, Limerick City Gallery of Art; *Hope Springs Eternal*, Dominic Berning, London (2003); *Drawing Biennale 2002*, Galleri F15, Jeløya, Norway; *ARCO 2002*, Madrid; *B Hotel*, PS1 Contemporary Art Center, New York (2002); *ev·a 2001*, Limerick City Gallery of Art; National Collection of Contemporary Drawing, LCGA (2001). Lives and works in London.

Unexpected Elsewhere

2003, DVD video on LCD screens with drawings
venue: City Hall

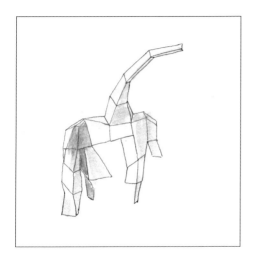

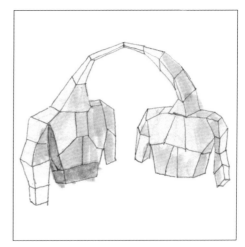

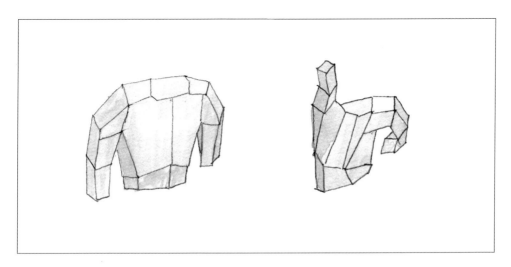

Christine Mackey

Born in Co Kilkenny in 1968. Graduated with an MA in Visual Performance from Dartington College of Arts, Devon, in 2002. Currently on an artist's work programme at the Irish Museum of Modern Art, Dublin. Recent solo exhibitions include: *The Process Room*, IMMA, Dublin (2004); Belltable Arts Centre, Limerick (2003); Model Arts & Niland Gallery, Sligo (2003). Group exhibitions include: *Small Victories*, Modest Contemporary Art Projects, Chicago (2004); Live Art Event, Fringe Festival Studio, Dublin (2003); *US LIVE*, WAH Center, New York, and 5th Gallery, Dublin (2003). Shortlisted for AIB Young Artist Award, 2004. Forthcoming projects include Eigse Arts Festival, Carlow (2004), and a residency and exhibition in Costa Rica (2004-05) as a result of winning the Open award at *ev·a 2003*, Limerick. Lives and works in Co Leitrim.

I began in July 2003 by collecting 1,000 jam jars from people in my local area. The whole process, from visiting people, collection of jars, to washing, to drawing, to presentation is imperative to the project. Recycling becomes the 'method'[1] of doing, and also the matter. A further 2,000 jam jars were donated by Alpack, a recycling company in Dublin.

The drawings for this project were sourced in *The Morphology of Forms*, a book published in the 1800s. I began by copying the original drawing onto the jam-pot lid covers. I then photocopied each diagram, increasing the scale from 100% to 200%, on up to 400%, and copied all of the results on to the jam-pot lid covers using white ink. I continue the whole process over and over again so that the original diagram is no longer legible as a unique drawing. I am working with intensification of scale on a continuous basis, with each round of drawings worked from the previous round of photocopying. My intention is to upset the original through the mechanical process of the photocopy machine. A synthesis of the hand-drawn and the machine ironically twisted into the copy both as source and result.

The work draws attention to a number of issues – diagram as 'ready-made';[1] questioning the source of originality; product of consumption into the reproduction of artwork; public participation; 'models of sociality'; democratisation of the art object; and ownership of work.

[1] Nicolas Bourriaud, *Post Production*, 2000
[2] Quote from an essay by John Miller, 'Drawings that question diagrams', 1977-98

Collection: *'Select a diagram from a book, copy it by hand. Repeat this procedure over and over. Compile the results and present them as a...'*[2]

2003, glass jars with mixed media on plastic, dimensions variable
venue: Church Gallery, Limerick School of Art & Design

Katrina Maguire

Born in Derry. Studied painting at Chelsea School of Art, London, and recently graduated with an MA in Fine Art (media) from the National College of Art & Design, Dublin. Currently based in Temple Bar Gallery & Studios. Has exhibited extensively in Ireland and abroad; recent exhibitions include: *Haunted*, City Art Centre, Dublin; *Bedding Out*, Dun Laoghaire-Rathdown County Council; *A way a lone a last a loved a long*, Museum of Contemporary Art, Zagreb, Croatia; *draw'ing-room*, Temple Bar Gallery & Studios, Dublin; *D-sixteen*, Static Models Gallery, Liverpool; *Two Seas*, Old Museum Arts Centre, Belfast. Forthcoming projects (2004-05) include video work at the Context Gallery, Derry. Lives and works in Dublin.

Picture: a visible or visual image. A cinematograph film: (in pl) a cinematograph show or the building in which it is given. v.t. to depict, represent in a picture: to form a likeness of in the mind: to describe vividly in words.

Pictured-turing-tures: To make a visible representation or picture. To form a mental image of; visualise.

Picture-house-place: a building for cinematograph shows.

— *Readers' Digest Great Illustrated Dictionary* (RDA, 1984)

Studying a man recounting memories from his youth, *Picture House* suggests a theatre space. Animated and expressive, the raconteur describes his experiences of going to a rural picture house during the late 1940s. The project examines the nature of how memories are described and communicated. Maguire provides the dialogue and the setting through the medium of storytelling and video imagery, allowing the audience to imagine their own version of events.

Picture House
video installation of two synchronised DVD projections, 8 mins
venue: Limerick City Gallery of Art

Dorit Margreiter

Produces installations, photographs and videos dealing with aspects of representation in gender, architecture and film. Graduated from the University for Applied Arts, Vienna (1992). Artist in residence in Tokyo (1996); Kuenstlerhaus Bethanien, Berlin (1998-99); MAK Center for Art & Architecture, Los Angeles (2001). Solo exhibitions include: *Event Horizon*, Museum of Modern Art, Vienna (2004) and Galerie Krobath Wimmer, Vienna (2002); *Short Hills*, Plattform, Berlin (2001); *Everyday Life*, Galerie im Taxispalais, Innsbruck (2001). Has participated in group shows internationally. In 2001 she developed the concept for the series *The Experiment* at Vienna Secession, and curated *Browsing Art* at the Generali Foundation in Vienna. Awarded the Otto Mauer Award in 2002, and Award of the City of Vienna in 2004. Lives and works in Vienna and Los Angeles.

Untitled (Los Angeles)
2004, lambda prints, 30 x 40 cm
(courtesy Galerie Krobath Wimmer, Vienna)
venue: Limerick City Gallery of Art

Untitled (Las Vegas)
2004, lambda prints, 30 x 40 cm

114

Maxine Mason

Born in London. Completed an MA at the Royal College of Art, London (1992-94). Selected exhibitions: *Can't Fake the Feeling*, K3, Zurich (2003); *Portrait of Francis Bacon as an Exquisite Corpse*, 39 Gallery, London (2003); Braziers International Artists Workshop, Braziers, Oxfordshire (2003); *Masstab eins zu eins*, Anker/K3, Switzerland (2003); *Please Take One*, 39 Gallery, London (2003); *Suicide is Painless*, On the Rocks, London (2003); *Centrefold*, Bart Wells Institute, London (2002); *New Paintings*, Falmouth College of Art & Design (2001); *What She Wants*, Laure Genillard, London (2000); *Hard Candy*, Galerie Wieland, Berlin (2000); *Outdoors*, Foyles Gallery, London (2000); *Coffee & TV*, Vilma Gold, London (1999); *X-sights*, Lancester Gallery, Coventry (1999). Lives and works in London.

Keep-on is an installation built on site. It is one of a series of dance floors that I have recently built on location, growing out of my interest in underground cubs and DJ culture.

With this installation I am concerned with audience and viewer participation, and attempting to make something more interactive, where art extends into the social arena. I am less interested in it functioning as an art object or commodity, but as something that can be engaged with on a more practical as well as emotional level.

The dance floor has always been a site of participatory activity, performance and drama. At times it is a stage, and at other times the object of voyeuristic activity. I am interested in building on the atmosphere and associations that the dance floor already creates, using the language and technologies of the club and disco.

Under the floor is a composed sound piece made especially for this piece. This is a 'mash up', using audio sampling techniques to extract key moments and intros from well-known disco and pop tunes. These are cut, pasted and layered together to create a frustrating build of music that vibrates from beneath in an attempt to draw the viewer on to the dance floor surface.

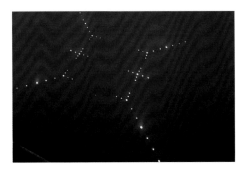

Keep-On

2004, installation, 4' x 4' dance floor, CD, speakers, disco ball, smoke machine, disco lights
(produced with the assistance of ev·a)
venue: disused shop at the Potato Market

Aisling O'Beirn

Has participated in exhibitions in Ireland and internationally, including *Home Town*, Galway (2003); *Think Over*, Rialto Santambrogio, Rome (2003); *Urban Projects*, Golden Thread Gallery, Belfast (2002); Cetinje Biennial, Montenegro (2002); *Artfront-Waterfront*, Staten Island Ferry Terminal (2002); *Temporary Provisions*, Ormeau Baths, Belfast (2001); *Bureau*, Dun Laoghaire-Rathdown County Council (1999); *Urban Control 1*, Forum Stadzpark, Graz, Austria (1999); *Planetarium*, Temple Bar Gallery, Dublin (1998); *Panorama*, Tiergarten, Berlin (1998); *British Architecture In Ireland*, Puffin Room, New York (1998); *Cultivate*, Context Gallery, Derry (1997); *Wandering Sailor*, Triskel Arts Centre, Cork (1996). Details of previous work on www.aislingobeirn.fsnet.co.uk. Lives and works in Belfast.

This project consists of a series of street signs of Limerick nicknames. The signs take a similar form to the city's official street signs, and are sited in their respective locations around the city for the duration of the exhibition. A map with a key to the signs and information on the background to the nicknames is located in the gallery. The map uses some of the same visual iconography found in official street signage and maps.

I am presenting the type of information that does not appear on official city maps or signage. *Limerick Nicknames* aims to examine how people's nicknames for places and landmarks help describe the urban fabric of the city. It is also concerned with how naming is a way of claiming local knowledge, and how maps become like editorial documents where select information is included or left out according to the map's function.

Limerick Nicknames

2004, vinyl on aluminium, various locations in city centre

(produced with the assistance of ev⁺a) (with thanks to Mike Finn, Maura Ní Ghadha, Áine Nic Giolla Coda, Anne Kelly, Tom Keogh, Étaín MacConghail, Rory McDermott (Roads Dept), Annette Maloney, Mike Minnis, Deirdre Power, Paddy Power, Seán Taylor, ev⁺a committee, WB Furniture, and Limerick City Council for nicknames, stories, contacts, translation and general help)

Roman Ondak

Born in Zilina, Slovakia, in 1966. Studied at the
Academy of Fine Arts, Bratislava, Slovakia (1988-
94). Solo exhibitions: Kunstverein Cologne (2004);
GB Agency, Paris (2003); Moderna Galerija, Zagreb
(2002); Ludwig Museum, Budapest (1999). Group
exhibitions: *That bodies speak has been known for
a long time*, Generali Foundation, Vienna (2004);
Utopia Station, 50th Venice Bienalle (2003); *Wir
mssen heute noch*, Kunstverein Cologne (2003);
Durchzug/Draft, Kunsthalle Zurich (2003); *I promise
it's political*, Ludwig Museum, Cologne (2002);
Ausgetrumt, Secession, Vienna (2001); *Manifesta
3*, Moderna Galerija, Ljubljana (2000); *After the
Wall*, Moderna Museet, Stockholm (1999);
Manifesta 1, Natural History Museum, Rotterdam
(1996). Lives and works in Bratislava, Slovakia.

Awaiting Enacted

2003-04, paper collage and metal table with glass,
73 x 230 x 62 cm
venue: Limerick City Gallery of Art

Vanessa O'Reilly

Born in Mexico in 1972. Educated at the Crawford College of Art & Design, Cork; Limerick School of Art & Design; and Chelsea College of Art London. Invited artist at Fabrica, a residency sponsored by Benetton (1996-97). Has just completed an international residency at the Gasworks, London. Exhibitions include: Bienal de la Havana, Cuba (2003); *Eurojet Futures 2002*, RHA Gallagher Gallery, Dublin; *Big Torino*, Turin Biennale; *Gasterbeiter at 2YK*, Kunstfabrik, Berlin; *ev·a 2002 heroes + holies*, Limerick; *ev·a 2001 expanded*, Limerick. First UK solo exhibition, *Premises*, at Milch Gallery London in 2002. Forthcoming projects for 2004: *No Respect*, Dublin; Butler Gallery, Kilkenny. Lives and works in London.

Through the amalgamation of the diverse forms and strategies within her work, Vanessa O'Reilly encourages an open-ended, non-didactic practice and interaction with her audience. She is interested in the flexibility of being able to look at a situation and then define herself within that context, rather than working on anything that has to be defined in terms of its place of origin, where it has been made, or where the idea arose. Decisions for the work have been made in video, photography, drawing and sculpture, and have predominantly been presented in site and context-specific situations and installations. O'Reilly is undoubtedly an optimist who demands a reaction to her individualistic affiliation to the world at large. She is also an observer whose work is often connected to making a sense of place ... an intrinsic quality to the work is a nomadic sensibility, an understanding of the shifting nature of possibilities of display, as well as the paradigms that surround and create each and every opportunity.

— Lisa Panting
from catalogue for *Premises* (Milch Gallery, London, 2002)

Feux d'Artifice

2003-04, light, sound and coloured gel installation
(the sounds are recordings of the artist's voice/mouth imitating a distant fireworks display)
venue: Chamber of Commerce, O'Connell Street

Alan Phelan

Born in Dublin in 1968. Studied at Dublin City University (BA), Glasnevin, Dublin, and Rochester Institute of Technology (MFA), Rochester, NY. Selected solo / two-person exhibitions: Limerick City Gallery (2000); Triskel Arts Centre, Cork (2000); Arthouse (with Jim Dingilian), Dublin (1998). Group exhibitions and projects include: *Country*, Ljubljana (2004); *Tulca Festival of Visual Arts*, Galway Arts Centre (2003); *Appendiks 1*, Thiemers Magasin, Copenhagen (2003); *Affinity Archive*, Metropolitan Complex, Dublin (2003); *Permaculture*, Project, Dublin (2003); *Crawford Open 3*, Crawford Gallery, Cork (2002); *Perspective 2002*, Ormeau Baths Gallery, Belfast (2002); *Love 2 Love*, Catalyst Arts, Belfast (2002); *Fabulations of Form*, Arthouse, Dublin (2002); *Stand Fast Dick and Jane* (co-curated with Tom Keogh), Project, Dublin (2001). Lives and works in Dublin.

Dear Zdenka

You are probably almost finished your selection for ev⁺a by now and I know this is quite late getting to you. Apologies. I had an idea for a proposal but actually fell sick with flu over the last week, and as I went off-colour so did my initial concept. Nevertheless, suddenly, as I recover, it seems like something that may actually be useful to you and so I am sending you this short proposal. The idea came to me after attending some talks at last year's ev⁺a. Many issues surrounding the exhibition were discussed in a two-day informal session. One of the things I had noted was how the interpretative devices used for the show always seemed quite poor during the exhibition. The catalogue is normally published towards the end of the exhibition, and in the meantime there is not a lot that comes between the viewers and the art. This is not necessarily a bad thing.

My idea was to write interpretative text panels for all the exhibition spaces in ev⁺a. They could be written in conjunction with the curator, but I would prefer it to be a commentary on their selection rather than a collaborative initiative. The texts would be short, pithy and not entirely descriptive. Rather than explain everything, they would add an additional narrative to the selection (while also guiding viewers towards thinking about the work on display). The writing would need to be done in the two weeks running up to the opening of the show so that the panels could quickly go through graphic design production and installation.

Regarding my experience, I have exhibited in Limerick City Gallery several times, as part of ev⁺a and also with a solo exhibition in 2000. I write a regular column for the SSI Visual Artists Newsletter and am a member of AICA. I have also visited Slovenia recently and there should have been a twist to this proposal but it didn't happen due to this damn flu. Hope you have time to consider this and that we get a chance to discuss this further.

Best regards,
Alan Phelan

Untitled (text panels)
2004, 28 ink-jet prints mounted on PVC, various sizes
(the texts are reprinted on pages 162-171)

Eline McGeorge
Unexpected Elsewhere

Eline McGeorge is from Norway but lives in London and exhibited in last year's exhibition. Her practice is concerned with the act of drawing and despite the use of animation they are understood more as moving stills. The work combines various types of drawing and small narratives, delicately exploring a range of tiny tragedies and triumphs. Each work starts as a still drawing on paper or computer and is sparingly animated to become short sequences. The impossible suddenly becomes possible, subtly shifting the mundane events and actions, moving between wall, paper and screens. This provides a flexible space to consider not only the act of drawing but also the physical properties of the everyday.

Ayse Erkmen
Untitled

Ayse Erkmen is from Turkey but lives in Germany. Her work takes many forms that range from performances to installations. In one work she has placed gates at the entrance of museums, in another she made subtle changes to the architecture and lighting of gallery rooms. In this work she uses a font based on one from an old typewriter to possibly explore Irish literary history. Instead of using any specific writer or quote the sentence used is one that graphic designers or font design companies to show each letter of the alphabet in a nonsense series of words. This humorously points to willingness to share in a tradition and feeling excluded from it especially since she was unable to obtain a visa to install the exhibit.

Anri Sala

Born in Tirana, Albania in 1974. Education: BA, National Academy of Arts, Tirana (1992-96); Ecole Nationale Supérieure des Arts Décoratifs, Paris (1996-98); postgraduate studies in film directing, Studio National des Arts Contemporains, Tourcoing (1998-2000). Solo and two-person exhibitions: Hauser & Wirth Gallery, London (2004); Musée d'Art Moderne, Paris; Deichtorhallen Hamburg; Art Institute of Chicago (2004); Kunsthalle Wien, Vienna (2003); *All Gone*, Residence-Project Gallery at CCA, Kitakyushu, Japan (2003); *Amplified Absorbers*, Galerie Hauser & Wirth, Zurich (2002); *Concentrations*, Dallas Museum of Art (2002); *It has been raining here*, Galerie Chantal Crousel, Paris (2001); Rüdiger Schöttle Gallery (with Martin Creed), Munich (2001); *Unlimited nl-4* (with Christian Jankowski), DeAppel, Amsterdam (2000). Lives and works in Paris.

The camera moves through the street by night, and partly by day, along the houses whose façades have been partly coloured red, blue, yellow, green, etc. In the foreground are torn-up streets and garbage. You can hear a conversation between the artist and the mayor of the city – a politician with cultural and educational concerns.

The story is this: after the political change, the apartments had been enlarged individually by the inhabitants since the situation was so anarchic that there were no laws that could have forbidden it. Walls had been torn down and balconies enlarged, so that every family could get as much space as possible. The façades looked awful – deformed, grey and damaged. The situation corresponded to the mentality of the people. Nobody was interested in how their house looked from the outside. More important was how they looked inside. There was no sense of community. The mayor photographed the façades and decided on a colour concept for certain parts. Most of the inhabitants did not like the idea, but agreed to let the intervention continue. For the first time, a sense of community was noticeable, and over time, people committed more and more to the idea, and started to communicate with each other and with the mayor.

What is interesting here is not so much the aesthetic aspect of the intervention – the renovation of the façades and the improvement of the street scene – but rather the social experiment. The most fascinating thing is the fact that such a minimal effort made possible a big change in self-perception and, more importantly, in their perception of community.

Dammi i Colori

2003, video projection with sound, 15^1/$_2$ mins
(courtesy the artist and Hauser & Wirth, Zurich / London)
venue: Limerick City Gallery of Art

Efrat Shvily

Born in Jerusalem in 1955. Education: studied
photography, Meimad and Bezalel Academies,
Israel; BA Political Science, Bar-Ilan University,
Israel; MA, Oxford University. Solo shows: Centre
de la Photographie, Geneva (2002); Galerie Martine
& Thibault de la Chatre, Paris (2000); School of Art,
Beit Berl College, Kfar Saba (1999); *The Israeli
Season in France*, Le Quartier Center for
Contemporary Art, Quimper (1998); Herzlia
Museum, Herzlia (1995); *Photographs from Israel*,
Bezalel Academy, Jerusalem (1993). Group
exhibitions include: *Blickverbindung*,
Produzentengalerie, Hamburg (2004); *Poetic
Justice*, Istanbul Biennial (2003); *Dreams and
Conflicts: The Viewer's Dictatorship*, Venice
Biennale (2003); *Nos/Ostros: Identity and
Otherness*, PhotoEspana, Madrid (2003); *Based on
True Stories*, Rotterdam and São Paulo (2002-03).

Have no fear at all
2003, DVD video projection, 13 mins
(courtesy of Sommer Contemporary Art, Tel Aviv)
venue: St Mary's Cathedral

Nedko, Veselina & Dimitar Solakov

NEDKO SOLAKOV was born in Cherven Briag, Bulgaria, in 1957. Has exhibited extensively in Europe and the United States, including biennales in Venice, Istanbul, São Paulo, Rotterdam, Gwangju, Lyon, and *Sonsbeek 9*, Arnhem. Recently he had solo shows at Museu do Chiado, Lisbon; Stichting DeAppel, Amsterdam; CCA Kitakyushu, Japan; Museo Nacional Centro de Arte Reina Sofia, Madrid, Israel Museum, Jerusalem. Touring retrospective to Luxembourg, Malmo Linz in 2004-05. Lives and works in Sofia. VESELINA and DIMITAR, the artist's children, were born in Sofia in 1986 and 1987. Even though they took part in many of their father's earlier projects, *Family Business* is the first one where they present their own works following his invitation to replace him at Invited ev⁺a.

FAMILY BUSINESS

I am not quite sure that I understand my teenage children's system of values

I keep trying to keep in touch with the world of our 17-year-old daughter Veselina and our 16-year-old son Dimitar, but, so far, even though we haven't had serious conflicts or misunderstandings, I can hardly say I can manage it. On the other hand, my wife, as their mother, seems much better at it.

Recently I decided to try to approach the problem from the other way around - to gently force my children into more direct contact with my system of values, which is, no doubt, the proper, the better system compared to theirs. Being an artist nowadays is not easy and the first lesson I had to start with was to show them first hand how hard it is for an artist to participate in an exhibition on the other far edge of Europe, in Ireland. So, I extended the ev+a invitation which had originally been sent to me to my children.

They accepted with relative pleasure and quickly came up with ideas for their works. My son wants an old TV set displayed, switched on, but without any antenna or cable connections, so that the screen will show that buzzing, snowfall image. The title is "Star Wars". My daughter, who is a devoted fan of Winnie the Pooh, has her room in Sofia packed with numerous items related to him and his friends. She would like the ev+a organizers in Limerick to purchase the biggest possible Winnie the Pooh doll which her collection lacks because her constantly travelling father never really has the guts to carry such a huge doll back home. She intends to arrange it in a suitable way next to "Star Wars." And of course, after the exhibition ends the giant bear is to be shipped back to her in Sofia.

Ideally I am not supposed to join them for the installation of their pieces and for the opening of ev+a 2004 Imagine Limerick. They should travel and meet all possible obstacles on their own. But they are after all still small kids and daddy has to be with them, even though it seems they already have a good knowledge of some proper things that, in time, may become proper values once they put them in a system.

Family Business
2004, installation
venue: Limerick City Gallery of Art

Family Business

I am not quite sure that I understand my teenage children's system of values.

I keep trying to keep in touch with the world of our 17-year-old daughter Veselina and our 16-year-old son Dimitar, but, so far, even though we haven't had serious conflicts or misunderstandings, I can hardly say I can manage it. On the other hand, my wife, as their mother, seems much better at it.

Recently I decided to try to approach the problem from the other way around - to gently force my children into more direct contact with my system of values, which is, no doubt, the proper, the better system compared to theirs. Being an artist nowadays is not easy and the first lesson I had to start with was to show them first hand how hard it is for an artist to participate in an exhibition on the other far edge of Europe, in Ireland. So, I extended the EV+A invitation which had originally been sent to me to my children.

They accepted with relative pleasure and quickly came up with ideas for their works. My son wants an old TV set displayed, switched on, but without any antenna or cable connections, so that the screen will show that buzzing, snowfall image. The title is "Star Wars". My daughter, who is a devoted fan of Winnie the Pooh, has her room in Sofia packed with numerous items related to him and his friends. She would like the ev+a organizers in Limerick to purchase the biggest possible Winnie the Pooh doll which her collection lacks because her constantly travelling father never really has the guts to carry such a huge doll back home. She intends to arrange it in a suitable way next to "Star Wars." And of course, after the exhibition ends the giant bear is to be shipped back to her in Sofia.

Ideally I am not supposed to join them for the installation of their pieces and for the opening of ev+a 2004 Imagine Limerick. They should travel and meet all possible obstacles on their own. But they are after all still small kids and daddy has to be with them, even though it seems they already have a good knowledge of some proper things that, in time, may become proper values once they put them in a system.

Malin Ståhl

Born in Sweden in 1975. Education: Cultural Studies, Linköping University, Sweden (1995-97); BSc in Anthropology, East London University (1998-2001); MA in Creative Curating, Goldsmith's University, London (2001-03). Projects: participation with *Happy Pappy* artists' magazine in the UK exhibition *Transaction in Oslo* (2004); launched *Happy Pappy*, a new artist's magazine which she initiated and edited (2003); wrote text for *Works*, a book on the Swedish artist Johanna Billing (Milch, 2003); catalogue essay for artist Jennifer Espling, Royal College of Art, Stockholm (2003). Lives and works in London.

I'm interested in finding alternative ways of bringing different artists and their works together. In this investigation I place myself between the creator and facilitator. My projects tend to be initiated and materialised by me, while at the same time functioning as platforms for artists to make new works, demanding a different approach to their practices. My projects are mobile: they can be taken home; you can comfortably engage with them with your head rested on a pillow. I like to provide that comfort. At the same time I intend to provoke some kind of stirring in the brain – a reorganisation of thinking patterns retained through habit.

My interest in ev⁺a arose after having a conversation with an artist who had sent her proposal to ev⁺a. I was told that the concept was a secret, no one knew. Of course the curator would know, but I became interested in creating an independent link between the artists. For this purpose I decided to re-enact a round robin project carried out by Lucy Lippard in 1970, where she asked each artist to provide a situation within which the next artist was to work, so that the works created one cumulative, circular piece.

I proposed to invite all the artists chosen by the curator Zdenka Badovinac to participate in this round robin project. Organised in alphabetical order, the first artist will, in any means suitable for the printed page, create a situation for the following artist, who then responds, and his or her response sets the situation for the third, and so on, until all the artists have been included. The project is in process until all interested artists have submitted their contributions. You can follow the development of the project on line at www.eva.ie.

...an artwork as a situation as an artwork...
2004, web-site
venue: www.eva.ie

responses from Yuri Avvakumov (bottom left) and Sarah Browne (bottom right)

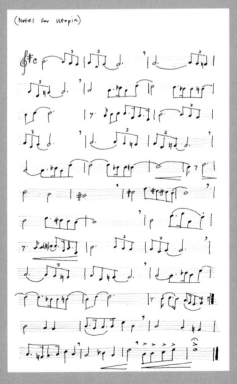

(Notes for Utopia)

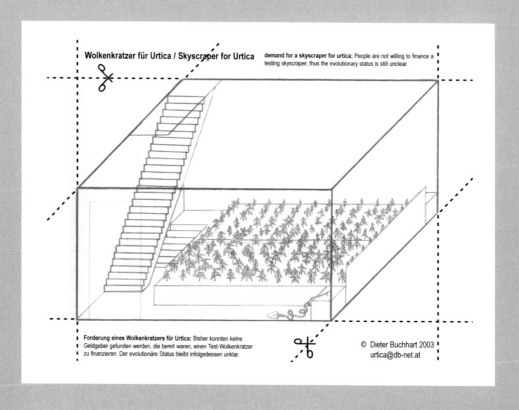

Wolkenkratzer für Urtica / Skyscraper for Urtica

demand for a skyscraper for urtica: People are not willing to finance a testing skyscraper, thus the evolutionary status is still unclear.

Forderung eines Wolkenkratzers für Urtica: Bisher konnten keine Geldgeber gefunden werden, die bereit waren, einen Test-Wolkenkratzer zu finanzieren. Der evolutionäre Status bleibt infolgedessen unklar.

© Dieter Buchhart 2003
urtica@db-net.at

Figure out my contribution to this project by spotting the adjustments I made to the drawing below:

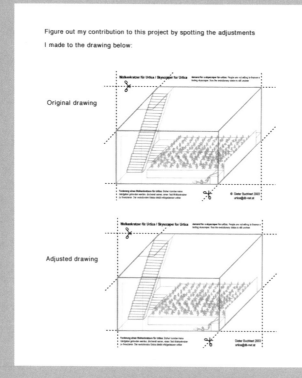

Original drawing

Adjusted drawing

...an artwork as a situation as an artwork...
2004, web-site

responses from Dieter Buchhart (above) and Gerard Byrne (below), and from Mark Cullen (opposite, top) and Ann Curran (bottom)

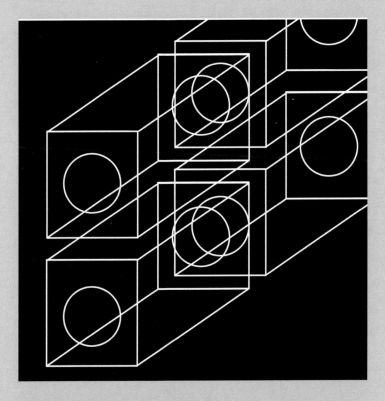

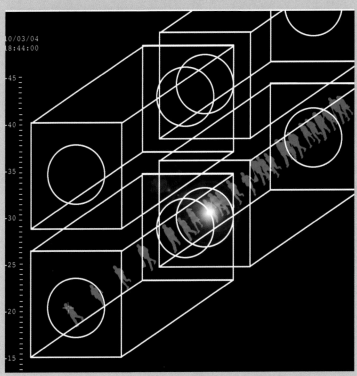

Mladen Stilinovic

Born in Belgrade in 1947. Selected solo exhibitions:
The Cynicism of the Poor, Museum of
Contemporary Art, Zagreb (2001); *White Absence*,
Glass Street Gallery, Melbourne, and Guss Fisher-
Gallery, Auckland (2001); Studio Josip Racic,
Zagreb (1997); CBD Gallery, Sydney (1996);
Geometry of Cakes, Moderna Galerija, Ljubljana
(1994). Selected group exhibitions: *In Search of
Balkania*, Neue Galerie, Graz (2003); *Be Creative!*,
Museum für Gestaltung, Zurich (2003); *By the
Way...*, Studio Racic, Zagreb (2003); *Here
Tomorrow*, Museum of Contemporary Art, Zagreb
(2002); *The Misfits*, Moscow, Berlin and Skopje
(2002); *Imaginary Balkans*, Site Gallery, Sheffield
(2002); *Ausgeträumt*, Seccession, Vienna (2002);
Six Artists, Moderna Galerija, Ljubljana (2001);
Chinese Whispers, Apex Art, New York (1999).
Lives and works in Zagreb.

Drei Tage bis zum Ende der Kunst
2003, installation, dimensions variable
venue: Church Gallery, Limerick School of Art & Design

Apolonija Sustersic

Born in Ljubljana, Slovenia, in 1965. Graduated from School of Architecture, University of Ljubljana (1992); postgraduate studies, Rijksakademie van Beeldende Kunsten, Amsterdam (1994-96). Professor at the Royal University College of Fine Arts, Stockholm, since 2003. Solo exhibitions: Community Research Project, Ibid Projects, London (2003); *Visual Cookie – Simulation Café*, Visual Carlow, Carlow (2002); *Unikat Club*, Kunstschafft, Witten (2002); *Eintritt*, Kunsteverin München, Munich (2002); *Light Therapy*, Bild Museet, Umeå (2001) and Moderna Museet Projekt, Stockholm (1999); *Home Design Service*, CASCO Projects, Utrecht (2001); *Non-Stop Video Club*, Mala galerija, Ljubljana (1999); *Entrance 1*, De Singel, Antwerp (1996); *Axiomatic Structures*, Gallery GT, Ljubljana (1992). Lives and works in Amsterdam, Stockholm and Ljubljana.

The Leidsche Rijn housing project is currently under construction in Utrecht. 30,000 houses are being built in what is the biggest housing development in the Netherlands and in Europe in the 90tis. The first buyers have already moved into their new homes however Leidsche Rijn will take at least another ten years to be finished. In the coming few years, Leidsche Rijn will be characterized by simultaneous living and building in a transitional phase.

project nr. 3015 is a video interview with the future residents of the new estate, talking about the interior of their own homes, which form the backdrop to the videos. They are projecting their thoughts and wishes onto the unfinished concrete structure, creating a fantasy home of their own.

project nr. 3015 was originally part of a bigger project *HOME.DESIGN.SERVICE*, produced with CASCO Projects in 2001.

project nr. 3015
2001, DVD video projection, 7¹/₂ mins
venue: Bourn Vincent Gallery, University of Limerick

Fiona Tan

Born in Pekan Baru, Indonesia, in 1966 to Australian and Chinese parents, and grew up in Australia. Graduated from Gerrit Rietveld Academie, Amsterdam, in 1992, and with a postgraduate degree from Rijksakademie van Beeldende Kunsten, Amsterdam, in 1997. Has exhibited widely since 1995, including Istanbul Biennial, Turkey (2003); Venice Biennale (2001); Yokohama Triennial, Japan (2001); *Documenta 11*, Kassel, Germany (2002). Awarded the Infinity Award for Art 2004 by the International Center of Photography, New York. Lives and works in Amsterdam.

News from the near future

2003, DVD projection, 18 mins
(courtesy the artist and Frith Street Gallery, London)
venue: Limerick City Gallery of Art

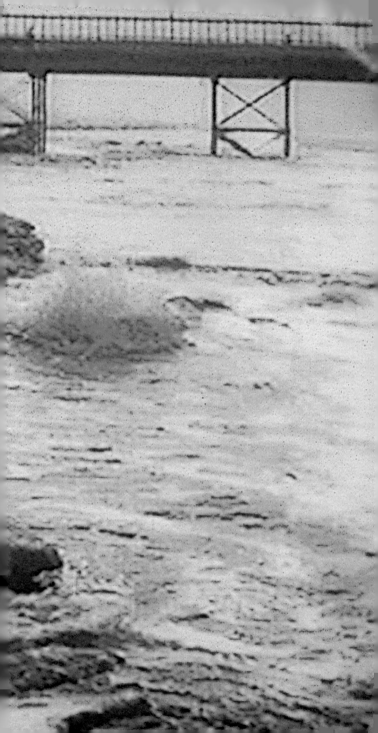

Sally Timmons

Born in Dublin. Education: BA Fine Art, National College of Art & Design, Dublin (1991-95); BA Photography, DIT Photography & Digital Imaging Studio, Dublin (1999-2003). Recently exhibited video work in *Perspective 2003*, Ormeau Baths Gallery, Belfast; *Seeing By Wireless*, Shot by the Sea Film Festival, Hastings (2003); *Crawford Open 4*, Crawford Gallery, Cork (2003). Photography and site-specific exhibitions include *10 x 10*, Right Angle Gallery, Paris (2002), *Via*, off-site group show, Dublin (2002); *The Apartment*, New York (2001). One of three founding members of the artist-led initiative *Via*, planning their third curatorial venture in April 2004. Lives and works in Dublin.

The ventriloquist that balances corpses on its knee, that gives speech to silence, and transforms bones and blood into reminiscences, is none other than the historian. The keeper of the text. The teller of the story. The worker of mute mouths.

— Barbara Kruger / Phil Mariani, 1989

This short video loop illustrates the irreconcilable nature of a popular approach to storytelling. The process of recall happens in more than one way. This relates directly to the notion of history and how it is experienced and interpreted. This vignette serves to illustrate some of the processes which contribute to the construction of history through the use of memory and recall. It is not enough to have the capacity for memory in the form of historical archives and memory banks, because it is through the telling of a tale from the past in the future that a legacy will live on. History is increasingly experienced through popular media, which is considered by some a contributor to the amnesic culture within which we live now, and possibly in the future.

Message
2002, DVD on LCD monitor with cardboard storage box, 1¹/₂ mins
venue: Chamber of Commerce

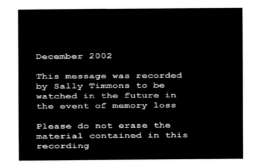

December 2002

This message was recorded by Sally Timmons to be watched in the future in the event of memory loss

Please do not erase the material contained in this recording

Aleksandra Vajd

Born in Maribor, Slovenia, in 1971. Education: MA, Faculty of Veterinary Medicine, Ljubljana, Slovenia (1997); MA Photography, FAMU – Academy of Performing Arts, Prague (2001); currently studying for PhD in the theory of photography at FAMU, Prague. Solo exhibitions: *Second Kiss*, PHOTO Gallery, Sarajevo (2001); *ZONA*, Galerie K, Bratislava, Slovakia (2001); *Crumbs Upon the Sheet* and *Second Kiss*, Umetnostna Galerija Maribor, Maribor (2001); *Second Kiss* and *Minus seven and minus three and a half*, *Manifesta 3*, Moderna Galerija, Ljubljana (2000). Selected group exhibitions: *The Photographic Eye*, FotoFest, Houston, Texas (2003); *Osebno-Izrazno-Dokumentarno*, Moderna Galerija, Ljubljana (2003); *Balkan Konzulat, Sarajevo*, Graz, Austria (2003). Lives and works in Prague.

Lately I was going through my archive of negatives ... actually it started with a photo I made in the morgue when father died. Looking at the negatives of some past family events I found many photos of father lying in bed resting with eyes closed ... he looked dead 'cause the pose was very static ... maybe this was stupid 'cause to lie is a static action but there are different ways a persona can lie in bed ... the day before he died he was lying like this on his sofa and I was asking myself what if he is dead now ... it was as if
I were testing myself and getting ready for the moment.

Untitled
2003, ink-jet photographs on fabric, each 41 x 72 cm
(courtesy Rotor, Association for Contemporary Art, Graz, Austria)
venue: Limerick City Gallery of Art

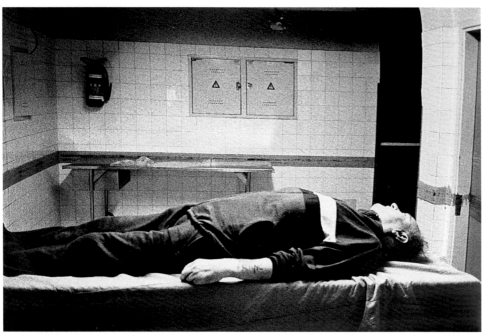

Anton Vidokle / Julieta Aranda

ANTON VIDOKLE was born in Moscow. His work has been recently featured in *Utopia Station*, Venice Biennale (2003); *Form Specific*, Moderna Galerija, Ljubljana; and at the Prague Biennale. Lives and works in New York. JULIETA ARANDA was born in Mexico City. Her work has been exhibited at the 7th Havana Biennale; Aldrich Museum of Contemporary Art, Connecticut; and La Panaderia, Mexico. Lives and works in New York.

Among the social uses of modernist abstraction, none is more contentious than that of public art – the last bastion, it has been said, of modernist controversy. What happens when this type of abstract, utopic, idealised geometry is projected into a public/social space is something artists Anton Vidokle and Julieta Aranda have set out to record in a tabloid newspaper they call *Popular Geometry*.

Reprinting a selection of the popular press's responses to abstract public sculpture – 'plop art,' as it was disparagingly termed in the 80s – *Popular Geometry* is the chronicle of a disarticulation and friction, of a language whose signification has largely evanesced and whose translation falls a beat or so short of conversion, where it becomes instead a kind of circus in which signs and gestures, aping sense, become parodical.

Popular Geometry is the broadsheet of this circus, with its range of largely negative (and unwittingly humorous) catalogue of articles from the last three decades culled from the Internet, as well as a cut-out insert of a do-it-yourself abstract geometric paper sculpture. But while *Popular Geometry*'s reprints may be chiefly negative in tone, it itself in no way aims to critique the abstract or public art that forms its subject. Rather, it functions to illuminate a disjunction that operates to decouple appearance and meaning, and within which 'the complex dance', in Joshua Decter's words, 'of art and politics, of culture and ideology, of form and function' endlessly and namelessly swirls.

Popular Geometry

2004, newspaper (edited by Anton Vidokle and Julieta Aranda)

(produced with the assistance of ev*a)

popular geometry

'CRANN SOILSE'

TOTAL WEIGHT 3,600 TONS

Over a past decade, the University of Limerick has been steadily building up a distinguished sculpture collection, but the unveiling of Sean Scully's Crann Soilse on 14 October 2003, marks a shift upwards in scale and ambition. This is the first sculpture made by Scully. Composed of hand-split cubes of stone, it takes the form of a wall, standing on a long earthen mound. The stones, alternately of cream limestone and black basalt, each measure 2'6" cubed. They are stacked in horizontal courses, three cubes wide by four high and forty long, forming a chequerboard pattern. Most of the stones are rough-faced, although one section, near the centre, is polished smooth. The total weight of the sculpture is estimated at over 3,600 tons.

Assembled without cement or mortar, Crann Soilse – the artist translates it as 'Wall of Light' – clearly references prehistoric structures such as the Mayan temples of Mexico, or Dun Aengus on the Aran Islands. Like much of Scully's work, Crann Soilse is about weight and lightness. It appears to float on its mound of grass, particularly at night when floodlit, but on closer viewing its great mass and weight become apparent. It is the key element in an architectural ensemble, designed by architects Shane de Blacam and John Meagher, which includes a yew hedge and two tall wooden masts. Set at a slight angle to the road that passes in front of the Plassey campus, the sculpture serves as a distinctive and unusual entrance marker to the University of Limerick.

Crann Soilse adheres to a fundamental dictum of Modernism, in that "it is what it is", and does not pretend to be something else. Perhaps its most important feature is that it is not just a facade of stone, fastened to a reinforced concrete core – instead, stones are used throughout, the chequerboard pattern extending through the length and breadth of the work. This inner core of stone, laid with the same care, attention and regularity as the visible outer layer of stones, is totally hidden.

An important intention of the artist was to create an object that he describes as the "opposite of fake". In doing so he evokes the aesthetic theories of John Ruskin, who also abhorred the use of stone veneers or fake masking. Scully's similar repudiation of the fascia or veneer involved 480 stones being quarried, hand-split into cubes and shipped from China and Portugal to Ireland. De Blacam visited the quarry in China where black basalt blocks were cut and hand-split into cubes for shipment to Ireland; he also visited Portugal, where white Moleanos limestone blocks were prepared in the same way... **(Cont. PG 3)**

BANGING MY HEAD AGAINST ANOTHER BRICK WALL

By Patricia Feehily
THE LIMERICK LEADER,
October 25, 2013

There was a time when a black and white brick wall erected as a monument to our hopes and aspirations, would have drawn the ire of a whole army of gobshites. Come to think of it a replica of an Isle of Man bank might better have reflected "the black and white severity of the Irish facade".

But where, for heaven's sake, have all the native cynics and natural philistines gone? Without them, all the fun is gone out of art and our culture heritage is filling up with strange monuments and spooky spires that surely will have distant descendants looking back at us in our own ancient evenings, and wondering what we were on about at all. What happened to the monumental genius of the people who built Newgrange?

Now, before I launch a fusillade of eminent international sculptor Sean Scully's Wall of Light unveiled last week at the entrance to UL, let me confess to my own lifelong state of unenlightenment - lest anyone should for a moment mistake me for a genuine art critic.

The first time I saw a print of Van Gogh's yellow chair I said to myself, this is awful. This fellow can't even draw. I might need a ruler, lest I, but I think I could do a lot better myself. That was a time when, looking even the remotest sense of perspective and desperately trying to attract the attention of the nun who taught us art in the Convent school in Nenagh, I traced enthusiastically everything in sight, but drew the line at the famous yellow chair. How dumb can one be?

I'm not getting any better either. At the moment, even the TV ads are artistically too complicated for me and their messages mostly elude me. But a psychologist friend has assured me that they are being received loud and clear in some unconscious part of my brain. Maybe, it's the same with the Wall of Light. Or maybe the reason why I'm disappointed with Limerick's latest monument is that I had been expecting a two - Crann Soilse.

Now there's nothing wrong with stone walls either. There's very much a part of our peasant identity and Crann Soilse means admitting the peasant in all of us, then I'm all for it, but I suspect it may be about pretending that we're something we're not. Unfortunately, some of us have met too many stone walls in life to be idly enthusiastic about one as massive or as thick as the Wall of Light. The other problem with the wall, is that I can't see the light apart from a row of artificial bulbs hidden in the ground at the base which are uncomfortably evocative of our declining neon culture. But then I have only seen it in the morning and at the setting of the sun.

The thing that really surprises me, however, is that nobody else seems the least bit inclined to take a verbal pot shot at the chequered edifice. They were very quick to condemn the "thing" of King John's Castle and the iron heart of July's roundabout. But in the groves of academe, only fools rush in to rant and rave, it's not as if we're lost our critical faculties however. It's just that we become more reverent in the glow of an intellectual aura.

What worries me is that everyone, it seems, has accepted without question this black and white wall as 'The light of our present hope and future possibility' as its creator described it.

Surely I can't be the only one who has been banging her head against a brick wall for too long not to appreciate the irony?

popular geometry

IMAGINE LIMERICK: ev+a 2004
REVOLVER, Archiv für aktuelle Kunst

Julieta Aranda & Anton Vidokle

157

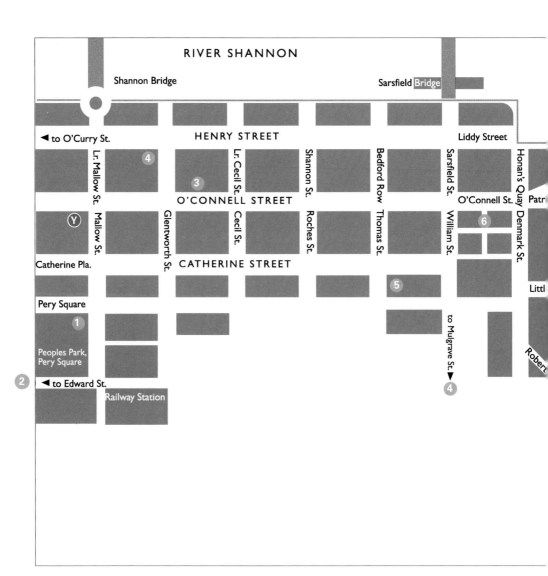

ARTISTS BY VENUE

1   **LIMERICK CITY
    GALLERY OF ART**
    Pery Square
    (open Mon-Fri, 10-6; Thurs
    10-7; Sat 10-5; Sun, 2-5)
    Yuri Avvakumov /
        Alyona Kirtsova
    Gerard Byrne
    Ben Cain / Tina

Gverovic
Mircea Cantor
Ann Curran
Alexandre da Cunha
Vadim Fishkin
Emily Jacir
Emilia & Ilya Kabakov
Ziga Kariz
Katrina Maguire
Dorit Margreiter
Roman Ondak

Anri Sala
Nedko, Veselina &
    Dimitar Solakov
Fiona Tan
Aleksandra Vajd

2   **SLATTERY'S PUB**
    50 Edward Street
    (outdoor work, best
    visibility at night)
    Michael Klien

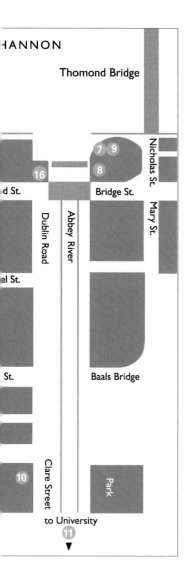

SHANNON

Thomond Bridge

Nicholas St.

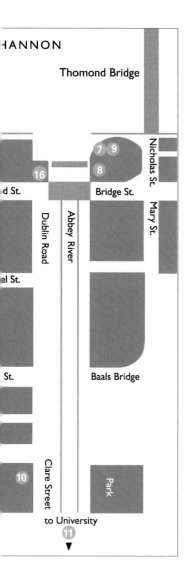

d St.

Bridge St.

Mary St.

Dublin Road

Abbey River

el St.

St.

Baals Bridge

Clare Street

Park

to University

Quay Shopping
Centre; Leonard's
Garage, Musgrave St
(office hours)
Mark Cullen /
    Brian Duggan

5   HALLA ÍDE
Thomas Street
(office hours)
Phil Collins

6   CRUISE'S STREET
(temporary work/
performance)
Johanna Kandl

7   TRACES OF FIRE
city wide tracking project;
map references located in
the Glazed Street, City Hall
Volkmar Klien /
    Edward Lear

8   ST MARY'S
    CATHEDRAL
Bridge Street
(open Mon-Fri, 10-4.30;
Sat-Sun, 10-1)
Efrat Shvily

9   CITY HALL
    EXHIBITION AREA
Merchant's Quay
(open Mon-Fri, 10-5)
Janine Davidson
Ayse Erkmen
Leonora Hennessy
Eline McGeorge

10 CHURCH GALLERY
Limerick School of Art &
Design, Clare Street
(open Mon-Fri, 10.30-4.30)
Maja Bajevic

Sarah Browne
IRWIN
Borut Korosec
Paul McAree
Christine Mackey
Mladen Stilinovic

11 BOURN VINCENT
    GALLERY
Foundation Building,
University of Limerick
(open Mon-Fri, 10.30-4.30)
Carlos Amorales
Apolonija Sustersic

12 VARIOUS LOCATIONS
    (Limerick city centre)
Aisling O'Beirn

13 EXHIBITION VENUES
Alan Phelan

14 EV⁺A WEB-SITE
www.eva.ie
Malin Ståhl

15 LCGA AND OFF-SITE
    VENUES
Anton Vidokle /
    Julieta Aranda

16 POTATO MARKET
(open Mon-Fri, 10.30-5
by appointment)
Maxine Mason

Y   YOUNG EV⁺A 2004
13 March – 2 April
Belltable Arts Centre
69 O'Connell Street

---

3   CHAMBER OF
    COMMERCE
O'Connell Street
(open Mon-Fri, 11-4)
Dieter Buchhart
Vanessa O'Reilly
Sally Timmons

4   VARIOUS LOCATIONS
Limerick Youth Service,
Henry St; Arthur's

Admission free to all venues

cultural programme of eu presidency: limerick welcomes slovenia

Slovenia is situated in central Europe and borders the Adriatic Sea, Hungary, Austria, Croatia and Italy. A very mountainous country, with half of it covered by forests, it is rich in natural resources. The capital city of Ljubljana with its 276,000 inhabitants maintains the friendliness of a small town, and at the same time possesses all the characteristics of a metropolis. The main language spoken is Slovene, and the population of two million is made up mainly of Slovenes, as well as some Croats and Serbs.

The Cultural Programme for the Presidency of the European Union was set up to assist in making new friendships and new connections within the new Europe. One of the strands of the Irish presidency's Cultural Programme in 2004 is to feature an inward flow of contemporary artists from the accession countries through close association with arts festivals and companies nationwide. *ev⁺a 2004 – Imagine Limerick*, is one such collaboration. On the Day of Welcomes, Saturday 1st May, the participating ten towns and cities nationwide will host a programme of cultural activity linked to one of the new accession countries. Limerick is twinned with Slovenia, and through ev⁺a, Limerick welcomes the following Slovenian artists: Borut Korosec (pages 98-101), Aleksandra Vajd (pages 152-155), Vadim Fishkin (pages 68-71), IRWIN: Dusan Mandi, Miran Mohar, Andrej Savski, Roman Uranjek and Borut Vogelnik (pages 74-77), Ziga Kariz (pages 88-91) and Apolonija Sustersic (pages 144-145).

As well as the ongoing *ev⁺a 2004* exhibition – which was selected by Slovenian curator Zdenka Badovinac, and is open to the public until 23 May in venues across the city – ev⁺a – related Day of Welcomes events include:
• launch of the *ev⁺a 2004* book at Limerick City Gallery of Art on Friday 30 April at 8pm
• free bus tour of all *ev⁺a 2004* venues on Saturday 1 May, 11am (departing from LCGA).

The weekend also sees a host of other activities taking place, including:
• Procession of the Welcomes, with Serpentes (Slovenia) and Umbrella Project (Limerick)
• a wide range of musical events featuring Terra Folk and Jara Raja (Slovenia), Riverside Swing Band, Graffiti Classics, The Frames, Woodstar, and others
• a fireworks display from King John's Castle
• RiverFest Limerick Regatta
• River of Welcomes, with children from six schools embracing the Slovenian tradition of the Day of Lights on the Abbey River

day of
welcomes
may 1st 2004

imagine curating

ALAN PHELAN

see artist's statement pages 126-127

Alexandre da Cunha, *Fans* — Alexandre da Cunha lives in London but is from Brazil. He uses cheap, disposable or domestic objects to make sculptures that have, in the past, looked like orthopaedic devices or sporting equipment. Last summer I saw a photograph by Zarina Bhimji that reminds me somewhat of this installation. The picture was a big lightbox of a large empty room, most likely in Uganda, with the ceiling fans gathered around in the centre of the floor. This work has a similar feel of desperation with these collapsed fan propellers, made instead from discarded skateboards and hubcaps. The combination of automotive and youth culture in these works give the fans a whole different biography, of a life once lived elsewhere, now transformed into non-functioning objects, discarded but now decorative in a different way.

Yuri Avvakumov and Alyona Kirtsova, *Scale: Limerick(s)* — Yuri Avvakumov and Alonya Kirtsova are from Russia and have worked together on making these twelve photographs. Avvakumov trained as an architect in the 1980s and was part of a generation of 'paper architects' who emerged in the first decade of perestroika in the former USSR. These designers developed plans for buildings and structures which opposed official Soviet architecture by referencing early modernist designs and monuments, reintroducing a visual and cultural heritage that had been banished for decades. These often unrealised plans, however, were attempts to improve on the lived reality, offering more than just conceptual fancy. These photographs investigate in a similar way various spaces from around Limerick, assigning significance to unimportant or ephemeral aspects of the lived and social spaces around the city, provoking a rethink of places, structures and things.

Roman Ondak, *Awaiting Enacted* — Roman Ondak is from Slovakia and is known for interventions and performances where very little seemingly happens. By making small changes to everyday objects and places, he gently exposes the way things and situations are constructed both physically, metaphorically and socially. This practice has been termed by some writers as a 'microdrama', where small things shift, sometimes making a surprisingly big impact. In this piece the collaged newspaper clippings are all from Slovak newspapers, selected because they had photos of people waiting in queues, rearranged in a new layout.

This could be interpreted as a presentation of a stereotypical or even clichéd eastern European scene, with drab unhappy people suffering through an everlasting transitional era of post-communism. Considering this country is about to join the EU, this is more to do with an intentionally misrepresentative nostalgia, and is probably meant to be quite funny.

Anri Sala, *Dammi I Colori* — Anri Sala was born in Albania but now lives in Paris. His work deals with the enormous social, cultural and political changes that have happened in eastern Europe. Individual experiences and observations form a central part of his narratives, often revealing the disturbing realities and memories of recent conflicts and political systems. In this work, like other films, there is a metaphorical link made between private lives and the political situation in a country. The mayor of the city discusses how he decided on a colour coded system to mark various apartments that were altered without planning permission. This created a different sense of community, one which lacked any communal aesthetic or concern, linking now instead back to early modernist visual strategies, where they have suddenly become useful again.

Ziga Kariz, *Private future II* — Ziga Kariz represented Slovenia at the Venice Biennale last summer. These works are part of the same body of work called Terror=Decor, which draws parallels between terror, decorative house furniture and surveillance technology. In some of these works, digital cameras are inserted into the paintings, reversing the viewing process by having screens placed in people's homes to view the viewers. Here, however, the paintings sketch out a particular trajectory for early modern avant-garde design and art, which have been completely absorbed into commodity culture. These utopian movements, like the Dutch De Stijl group, thought they could liberate themselves from capitalism, and instead have been reduced to surfaces, meaningless colour patterns for highly designed interior spaces but still encoding the turbulent history of the previous century.

Katrina Maguire, *Picture House* — Katrina Maguire is from Derry and lives in Dublin. This video work is quite different from recent installations which have not involved video. This work provides a way of looking at the act of storytelling. The man talking about his memories of going to the movies is juxtaposed with images from the now disused cinema building. Positioned within the permanent collection of the gallery, this work additionally connects to the act of memory and how unreliable it can be sometimes. The story and the reality of what is described is not always the same or synchronised. This can produce new interpretations, new ways of looking at the world, especially when taken out of context or combined with unexpected elements like the surrounding paintings and photographs here from the collection.

Ben Cain and Tina Gverovic, *Untitled* — Ben Cain and Tina Gverovic have worked together on this piece. They both have family connections in Croatia and the UK. They are interested in making something you have to listen to and look at, something that acts as a kind of map or guide to the city of Limerick. This theatrical shadow and audio presentation explores the process of interpreting, translating and reading from tourist information and guide books. In this process the viewer can get lost or easily misdirected, wandering off into an imaginary city just like many tourists on their first day in a strange place. The work creates a vision of a new place, one tied to stereotype, memory and fiction.

Ann Curran, *Vertigo* — Ann Curran is from Dublin but also lived in the US for a while. Her work often addresses narrative and memory in various media, including photography, film and video. The photographs here resemble an array of postcards, and show various locations across the world, photographed with a web-cam on a single day. The images document a journey that happened on a computer monitor, travelling from Vienna to Los Angeles, across nine time zones. These web-cameras are generally used to provide weather reports for winter tourists, but also provide surveillance, surveying mountains, towns and indeed people. These images show how unreliable memory can be, how it can be replaced or invented, stretching and condensing time, forming a composite of a journey not taken.

Dorit Margreiter, *Los Angeles* — Dorit Margreiter, who is Austrian, has been making work that references American mass culture on and off for a few years now. One of her interests is to do with architecture, as in the photographs she has made here. She went looking for places around the city that looked like they could be Los Angeles or Las Vegas. She often references pieces of architecture or buildings in her installations, by combining sculptural elements with videos or photographs. The choice of these two American cities is in keeping with other work that references the confusion and influence that television has on our perception of the real world. Both of these places are where life is fabricated for entertainment. It's interesting, then, to see how this works in reverse, where the real world can be like the fiction of television.

Emily Jacir, *Entry Denied (a Concert in Jerusalem)* — Emily Jacir is from Palestine but lives in the US, and because she holds an American passport she can freely move between Palestine and Israel, which most Palestinians cannot. She has made work about the recent troubles and atrocities in her country, often memorialising specific events that pass through the western media unnoticed. Without making any excuses for the savagery of either side of the conflict, she explores instead a sense of loss that's beyond retribution, but also sometimes unavoidably sentimental. The story behind this work is described in the accompanying poster. This apparent joyous musical performance has a dark history and is a re-staging of a concert that was cancelled by the Israeli authorities for no other reason than there were outsiders helping the occupied peoples.

Ilya and Emilia Kabakov, *The twenty ways to get an apple listening to the music of Mozart* — Ilya and Emilia Kabakov are from Russia but now live in the US. Ilya Kabakov studied graphics and illustration and became one of the leading unofficial artists in the former Soviet Union. These artists worked against the system of social realism, and instead explored social and political issues through conceptual realities. His work developed into complex narrative installations in the early 1980s, and eventually he began collaborating with his wife Emilia on these large projects. As such, their work is known for its combination of words, images and objects, located in often humorous yet political settings and installations. The various ways to get the apple in this installation include schemes that are philosophical, magical, psychological, linguistic or just plain fun. The work is considered a commentary on unfulfilled promises, and the irony of human intellectual endeavours played out through the potential social gathering of the dinner party.

Nedko Solakov, *Family Business* — Nedko Solakov is from Bulgaria. His art can be mixture of anxiety, humour, compulsion and social critique. His installations can be hilarious, but are often also elusive interventions. He creates improbable situations from which to draw out a narrative that is played out through various objects and activities. With this work he proposed to explore the difference in value systems between himself and his teenage son and daughter. They were asked to determine what would be exhibited here, and then travel to Ireland to install the work. The popular culture references in the television and toy selected by the younger Solakovs do possibly point to a different understanding of the world. Sometimes it is not that difficult to expect your children to be conceptual artists, and with this piece, where the roles are exchanged, we see different generations possibly united through art.

Mircea Cantor, *The Landscape is Changing* — Mircea Cantor was born in Romania but lives in France. His work has dealt with travel as a complex range of experiences that have enabled a range of interventions and experiences. This often results in work that encourages cultural misunderstandings. He also co-founded the art journal *Version* which has a mixed bag of approaches highlighting the work of young artists. In his video, the street demonstrators are caught up with themselves rather than acting as a homogeneous group. They carry signs that have mirrored surfaces, reflecting, distorting and transforming the reality of the situation around them. The individuals struggle for expression in the same way that many contemporary artists do (especially in a large group show like this one).

Aleksandra Vajd, *Untitled* — Aleksandra Vajd is from Slovenia and lives between there and the Czech Republic. Her photographs are small and intimate, often suggesting narratives that are in diary form. The photographs displayed here are very personal, beginning with an image of her father laid out in a morgue. When she looked through her negatives recently she found many other similar images of him lying down, sometimes in bed with his eyes shut, almost looking dead. She mentions in a short text about these photographs that the day before he died she saw him lying very still and asked him jokingly if he was dead, she believed that she was testing herself for that imminent moment. Vajd is interested in how the things we most look forward to in life can also be the things we are most afraid of.

Vadim Fishkin, *Dictionary of Imaginary Places* — Vadim Fishkin was born in Russia but lives in Slovenia. His work is concerned with the problems of language. These are often dealt with in poetic ways, using a mixture of light, sound, and new technology. He likes to make links between the physical and metaphysical world, and sometimes even the supernatural. The ghost-like figures in the space have red lights that are activated by the sound of the speakers concealed within. The words recited are the names of places and countries, some familiar and some from the history of literature. These are graphically represented in the projection as rhythmic frequency waves. As a list of real and imagined places, delivered in two distorted voices, they act apparently as a haunting guidebook of the make-believe.

Fiona Tan, *News from the near future* — Fiona Tan was born in Indonesia but now lives in Holland. In fact she has a very mixed background which is very important in her work, her father is of Chinese origin and her mother is Australian. These multicultural roots are often referenced in her video installation work, looking at the relationships between ethnography and the social and personal formations of identity. This work uses film footage of water from the Filmmusem in Amsterdam. The various clips date from early documentary cinema through to modern video, ranging from calm waters to stormy seas. Despite being images of landscape, the video points towards the universality of water and its many contexts and uses, acting as a metaphor for the human condition, I guess.

Gerard Byrne, *Frank and Anne* — Gerard Byrne is from Dublin. He is best known for his photographs but also makes short films and videos. His photographs have a strong narrative structure, combining many genres to offer several readings of social and cultural issues or phenomena through precise sequencing and detailed captions or titles. His recent work has involved re-enactments of conversations that have only previously appeared in print or other formats. The performance on the night of the opening stages a surveillance operation using two actors who will mingle with the general public. The work is based around metaphysical films such as the 1974 Francis Ford Coppola film *The Conversation*, which raised many issues about the ethics of surveillance and cinematic voyeurism in post-Watergate America. Headphones will be available to listen to the actors' scripted conversations on the night, and a video will document the performance.

Maxine Mason, *Keep On* — Max Mason is from London. She studied painting, but has recently made several works that relate to her interest in music and social interaction. For this exhibition she has equipped a small space with a raised wooden dance floor, studded with light rods, a mirror ball, motion-sensitive lighting, and even a fog machine. Music is installed under the dance floor and provides soft vibrations underfoot, with a mix of classic dance intros. This abridged discotheque is located at the entrance to the Potato Market, beside City Hall. The work offers an intimate yet very social opportunity for people to get together, to get on the dance floor and perform. The participatory aspect of this work is very important, as the work is a functioning art object and social space.

Mark Cullen and Brian Duggan, *Short Shorts* — Mark Cullen and Brian Duggan are from Dublin, and together run Pallas Studios, renting studio spaces to artists and also organising exhibitions. Their project is located in three different places around the city: the Limerick Youth Service on Henry Street, the mall in Arthur's Quay Shopping Centre, and the showroom in Leonard's Motors on Musgrave Street, where videos will be on display. These were made in Tallaght last year when the artists worked with a group of young people from Killinarden, all who were 16 years old. The artists facilitated the making of eight short videos, with the participants writing and performing in these dramas. Placing the videos in these urban settings is in keeping with the spirit of their making, which was, in many ways, a reaction by the participants to current video works in art galleries. The dramas instead reference television and film genres of documentary, thriller and horror.

Johanna Kandl, *The Cleansing of the Temple* — Johanna Kandl is from Vienna and has worked a lot in eastern Europe. She often works in collaboration with her partner Helmut, generally on projects that deal with social problems. She is a painter who believes that painting can be a powerful tool, especially when using traditional styles, to transform the ordinary into something that can provoke dialogue or controversy. She has painted a mural on Quimper Square, which is the biblical scene of Christ throwing the sellers out of the temple. This can be understood as either a sentimental or confrontational approach to perceptions of Irish religious culture and the current consumer boom. It is certainly in keeping with her practice that often highlights problems, contrasting oversimplified slogans with complex realities.

Aisling O'Beirn, *Limerick Nicknames* — Aisling O'Beirn is from Galway but lives in Belfast. She is one of the few Irish artists to have exhibited in Slovenia, and has also worked on projects with Slovene artist Marjetica Potrc. Her work for this exhibition is located in ten places around the city. She has made alternative street signs that are based on old or popular nicknames. These signs are real references to the history of the city, but ones that have often been forgotten or erased from popular memory. The resemblance of the nameplates to official street signs can sometimes cause confusion but the work is about activating public spaces with questions, or at least acknowledgements, of their past and present. A map of the locations of all the signs is displayed in City Hall.

These artists – Max Mason, Mark Cullen and Brian Duggan, Johanna Kandl and Aisling O'Beirn – are part of the Zdenka Badovinac's *Imagine Realities* theme, along with Carlos Amorales, Yuri Avvakumov & Alyona Kirtsova, Dieter Buchhart, Gerard Byrne, Mircea Cantor, Phil Collins, Ann Curran, Alexandre da Cunha, Vadim Fishkin, Ben Cain and Tina Gverovic, Emily Jacir, Ilya and Emilia Kabakov, Ziga Kariz, Katrina Maguire, Dorit Margreiter, Roman Ondak, Anri Sala, Efrat Shvily, Nedko, Veselina & Dimitar Solakov, Apolonija Sustersic, Fiona Tan, Sally Timmons and Aleksandra Vajd. This theme deals with recognisable realities which are at the same time present, unknown or ambiguous.

Malin Ståhl, *an artwork as a situation as an artwork* — Malin Ståhl is from Sweden and has recently completed the creative curating course in Goldsmith's College, London. For her project she has asked other artists in the exhibition to contribute to a web site, hosted at www.eva.ie. The idea is based around a similar invitation the art critic Lucy Lippard made to some artists in 1970. She had been given some pages in an art journal and decided to ask artists to create a situation within which the next work was to be produced. Correspondence between the ev+a artists will create a separate exhibition of sorts, presented as a series of texts and images that can be printed off the internet. The idea began after she had a conversation with an artist who submitted to the open section of the exhibition and said that the concept submitted was a secret, one between the artist and the curator. For this work the secrets are between artists, who each produce a new work based on the previous private revelation or set of instructions.

Alan Phelan, *Untitled (text panels)* — Alan Phelan is from Dublin, but also lived in the US for a while. His work uses a variety of media concerning narrative and various strategies in which information and art is presented. For this exhibition text panels have been written about each artist and are positioned close to the artworks. The graphic for each panel is a smudged ev+a logo with a numbering system, not based on the number of artists but on the fact that this is the 28th annual exhibition. Working with and around the institution, these captions provide a service that the gallery cannot or has chosen not to perform, taking the place of the institution and curator as the authoritative voice, providing the audience with an interpretative strategy that is unofficial yet complicit with the institution.

These two artists – Malin Ståhl and Alan Phelan – are part of the Zdenka Badovinac's *Imagine Curating* theme, offering parallel curatorial strategies with the main concept for the exhibition.

Carlos Amorales, *Cascara* — Carlos Amorales is Mexican, but also lives in Amsterdam. His previous work with Mexican wrestlers has investigated both the vulgar and over-intellectualised, teaming up the likes of wrestler and social hero Superbarrio with Joan Jonas, to compare two ways in which theatrical action became a means of political action. His own wrestler character or persona, Amorales, has fought in rings erected in museums around the world, in self-reflective battles against himself and famous wrestlers. The word *cascara* when translated literally means 'peel', but in Mexican Spanish it also means a kind of football that is played on the streets. In the video two people play in the yard of a demolished building, and instead of using a ball they kick a plastic human scull around. This references the cruel aftermath of war where the victors often symbolically and in reality exorcise the enemy in playful, yet horrific ways.

Apolonija Sustersic, *project nr. 3015* — Apolonija Sustersic studied architecture in Ljubljana in the early 90s and went on to study art in Amsterdam where she now lives. Her work typifies recent relational art practices where audiences actively participate in situations and places constructed by the artist, previously, in her case, a juice bar, bike shed or cafe. This video is an interview with two future residents of a new social housing estate in Holland. The couple give a tour of their nearly completed home, discussing their perceptions and aspirations for this new neighbourhood. The Leidsche Rijn housing project will eventually contain 80,000 homes built over the next ten years, and like large building developments such as Ballymun in Dublin, residents have to live in a perpetual transitional environment where fantasy and reality intermingle with the planned and the impossible. The video is from a larger project called *HOME.DESIGN.SERVICE*, which offered a variety of advice services to incoming residents of the estate.

Phil Collins, *They Shoot Horses, Ramallah – the first hour* — Phil Collins is from England but lived in Belfast for a long time before moving to Hove. He makes photographs and videos that deal with the social and political effects of conflict and war. His work draws on the documentary tradition in photography and film, but acknowledges the unavoidable manipulation of people in this practice. Sometimes this results in capturing real moments of human suffering or indeed ecstasy; other times he openly directs situations and conversations through questions or editing, misrepresenting the subjects in a way that can reveal other things. In this new work he travelled to Palestine and asked nine young people to a dance marathon. As a place where everything is saturated in politics, this simple and fun task exposes a different and sometimes unseen humanity.

Janine Davidson, *Via Via* — Janine Davidson is from Dublin but was recently on a residency in South Africa. A fire at the studios where she worked in Johannesburg inspired these particular prints. A fellow artist was tragically killed in the blaze. Although the works are quite beautiful and formal, there are several social and cultural concerns that are reflected, literally, in the embossed maps and the shape of the journey through the streets stitched in gold thread. These are possibly acts of memory or memorial, not only to automobile culture, but to the human traffic through a modern and changing city.

Leonora Hennessy, *Untitled (TV Line)* — Leonora Hennessy is from Cork and has recently finished studies in Glasgow. Her work has used several different light and sound techniques to look at how places relate to objects. The three monitors in this work show television noise interrupted by coloured animated lines. The work is an attempt to redefine the act of drawing, stretching the parameters of what is even considered drawing or mark-making. The appearance of these dynamic lines on the screen of an otherwise dysfunctional or tuned-out television continues her investigation into landscape, space and a sense of place in ways that explore the possibilities of things that can be ordinary or insignificant.

Eline McGeorge, *Unexpected Elsewhere* — Eline McGeorge is from Norway but lives in London. She exhibited in last year's exhibition. Her practice is concerned with the act of drawing, and despite the use of animation they are understood more as moving stills. The work combines various types of drawing and small narratives, delicately exploring a range of tiny tragedies and triumphs. Each work starts as a still drawing on paper or computer, and is sparingly animated to become short sequences. The impossible suddenly becomes possible, subtly shifting the mundane events and actions, moving between wall, paper and screens. This provides a flexible space to consider not only the act of drawing, but also the physical properties of the everyday.

Ayse Erkmen, *Untitled* — Ayse Erkmen is from Turkey but lives in Germany. Her work takes many forms, ranging from performances to installations. In one work she has placed gates at the entrance to museums, in another she made subtle changes to the architecture and lighting of gallery rooms. In this work she uses a font based on one from an old typewriter possibly to explore Irish literary history. Instead of using any specific writer or quote, the sentence used is one that graphic designers or font design companies use to show each letter of the alphabet in a nonsense series of words. This humorously points to a willingness to share in a tradition and feeling excluded from it, especially since she was unable to obtain a visa to install the exhibit.

IRWIN, *Like to Like* — IRWIN are a group of five artists from Slovenia. They are also part of the NSK collective, which is a cross-disciplinary group that works between painting, music, theatre and design. Their work addresses the legacy of totalitarianism, actively using the symbols of various regimes and art movements to explore ideological structures in a variety of contexts. The photographs here document apparent interventions in the landscape. These are re-stagings of the activities of the Slovene conceptual group OHO, who were active in the 1960s and 70s. As with much work from that time, the only remaining evidence are instructions or poor-quality photographs. These reconstructions as large colour prints reinvest the performances with a contemporary clarity and weight.

Mladen Stilinovic, *Drei Tage bis zum Ende der Kunst* — Mladen Stilinovic was born in Belgrade but lives now in Zagreb. His work explores the tautologies of language and cultural value systems, often presenting inconsistent paradoxes that reveal repressed ideologies and politics. He has made many infamous statements regarding art, like one of the text pieces here which states that artists who do not speak English art are not artists. Language and humour are important here as the work uses several sources of texts to explore the end of art, as referenced in the title. The broken eggs in plastic bags and the potatoes are cheap or discounted food items in Croatia. Their eventual decomposition during the course of the exhibition provokes the social and political trauma inherent in the work, and, indeed, is symbolic of a changing Europe, one that currently marginalises his home country.

Sarah Browne, *The Gift* — Sarah Browne lives in Kildare and has recently completed her studies in Dublin, Krakow and Cyprus. She has worked on a variety of community and collaborative projects. The sofas on display are from a project where several others were re-upholstered in new patterns and given to people as gifts. A video was then made discussing the gift with each of the recipients. The sofas are a go-between for the artist and individuals who would not normally buy or have contact with art. These people have kindly lent their art-sofa to the exhibition, where they have been displayed as traditional sculptural objects despite the fact that they are really records of a social interaction.

Christine Mackey, *The Collection* — Christine Mackey is from Leitrim but also lives and works in Dublin. She was the winner of the open section of this exhibition last year. Her work continues to be concerned with the act of drawing as a social interaction. She has collected almost three thousand jam jars from people in her local area, diverting them from recycling bins, as well as getting a sizable donation from a recycling company. The drawings on the lids of the jars come from an early nineteenth-century book about the meaning associated with forms or lines. These have been copied several times by a photocopy machine, humanising the mechanical process through several generations of copying. As an exercise in social drawing, the work also references landscape in its arrangement, growing from the corner like crystalline basalt or a bacterial growth.

Paul McAree, *West* — Paul McAree is from Cork but lives in London. This installation of paintings looks at various aspects of Irish history through the history of painting. The style is reminiscent of Paul Henry or Jack B Yeats, but greatly enlarged and with little respect for classic framing and sequencing. The paintings reference the iconography of these other artists who contributed towards early Irish national and cultural identity by mirroring impressionist painting styles and content from continental Europe, placing peasants and working landscapes, like farmland, in the foreground. But even McAree's own paintings have been copied and re-rendered here, forcing us to think about how culture is constructed in a similar way to the IRWIN group who have combined several traditions and ideologies.

Maja Bajevic, *Untitled* — Maja Bajevic is from Bosnia but lives in Paris and Sarajevo. Much of her work is concerned with the human disaster of the recent troubles in the Balkan states. There are many highly charged symbols of these conflicts that are tied to socialism and totalitarianism. In her photographs and videos she often appears re-enacting particular events or situations. In this video she plays several characters who make several contradictory statements about religion. These provocative comments point towards the use of religion as a force for evil not good, where it acts a buffer zone or excuse for violence or hatred and a twisted notion of nationalism. In the context of this gallery, which was once a church, the work has a particular resonance that can additionally bring to mind the atrocities now associated with many religious institutions in Ireland.

Borut Korosec, *Commandments* — Borut Korosec is from Ljubljana. The work here is a computer programme that runs automatically. Across various panoramic views of a town, single words appear and on the bottom of the projection appears, the text from the Ten

Commandments. The views of buildings, streets and trees change to close-up views as different words appear on screen. Although there is no direct relationship between the single words and the Commandments, the tension or expectation that this creates is supposed to mirror the changing perspectives on the images of the town. This is a narrative that does not exist and can only be experienced by suffering through the work. It's like telling a story that nobody wants to listen to, maybe a lot like how religion is used by people for their own ends or the way preaching forces us to listen to a message that we might be uncomfortable with.

Sally Timmons, *Message* — Sally Timmons is from Dublin. She is involved with a public art project called *Via* that places artworks along a street in Dublin. It is an artist-lead initiative, similar to the early days of this exhibition that arose to give local artists an opportunity to exhibit contemporary art to local audiences. She studied photography and has an interest in visual archives. The video is like a forgotten archive box or message that has been found, which contains random information about an individual. This is not unlike the way archives function, as they contain mixed bits of information that, when retrieved and collated, contribute to a history that is always under construction, always being written and rewritten depending on what information is used. Here it is the history of an individual that is under reconstruction, but technology is letting her down, distorting the message, omitting crucial facts.

Dieter Buchhart, *how to build a house* — Dieter Buchhart is from Vienna where he also lives. He has shown quite recently in Cork. He has an interest in involving people in his artworks which explore how identity is created by rules or codes; this is influenced by his mixed studies in art and science. This video shows how even the construction of a building can parallel the construction of reality. The text that appears every so often is taken from a variety of sources to do with house building, drawing other political and media references into the simple act of building a wall, which, I guess, can be a metaphor.

Vanessa O'Reilly, *Feux d'Artifice* — Vanessa O'Reilly is from Tipperary but was born in Mexico and lives in London. Her interest lies in complex aspects of communication, where she often merges several narratives that can propose different ways of understanding a particular space, idea or thing. These small pieces of coloured gels on the fluorescent light tube above are kind of static or stripped down stand-ins for the fireworks that the artist is imitating in the speakers. The work re-presents something quite fantastic or spectacular as a provisional mix of visual and audio elements, poking fun at the literal translation from the French title, 'artificial fire', as well as having fun with these hazardous symbols of public celebration.

Efrat Shvily, *Have no fear at all* — Efrat Shvily is from Israel and works in photography and video. His work addresses the conflict in his country in powerful yet melancholic ways. A recent series of black and white photographs of Palestinian cabinet ministers portrayed a fledgling government, left incomplete with the outbreak of the second intifada. The work here is strangely fitting for the cathedral. Initially it would appear to be a group of people singing popular and folk songs, some of which sound like hymns in this religious setting, but these people are in fact Israeli settlers, singing songs that filled with aspirational and joyous celebration their new homes in confiscated lands.

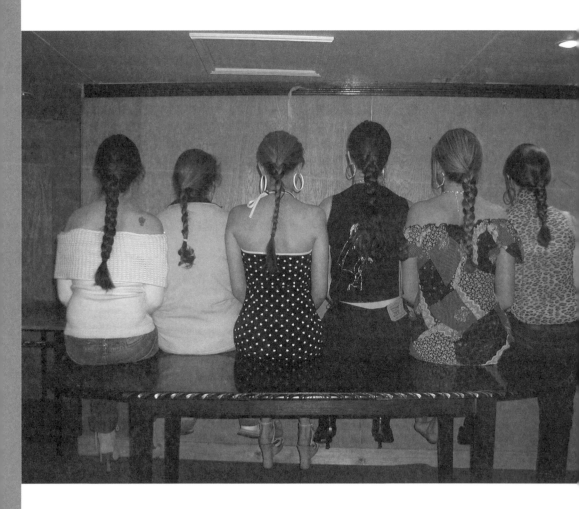

Better
Ireland
Programme

Making it possible

Amy O'Riordan, *Backs to the Future*, 2004

(opposite) young ev⁺a participants with Dick Sadlier,
Mayor of Limerick, at the opening of *ev⁺a 2004*

young ev⁺a

Young ev⁺a is the education and outreach project of ev⁺a, Ireland's premier exhibition of contemporary art held annually in Limerick. The project seeks to promote education, self-expression and social inclusion through contemporary art. Young ev⁺a this year featured the work of young people from the Limerick Travellers Development Group, St Mary's Youth Project, and the Southside Youth Initiative, who worked with artists Amy O'Riordan, Michael McLoughlin and Gillian Kenny respectively. This year's young ev⁺a was the most ambitious yet, thanks to the generous sponsorship of the AIB BANK BETTER IRELAND PROGRAMME.

> *A common thread running between the young ev⁺a projects this year is the interpretation of familiar spaces or actions and how the knowledge of the participants is at the centre of the artistic process. This made for collaborations in the real sense, as we all brought information, ways of working, stories and ideas that together resulted in the art work in the exhibition.*
>
> — Michael McLoughlin
> young ev⁺a artist co-ordinator, 2004

The resultant exhibition was held at the Belltable Arts Centre and featured paintings, drawings, photography, sound, sculpture and mixed-media installations which were a response to the groups' environments and experiences.

The young ev⁺a programme specifically for young people was developed in 1986 in conjunction with ev⁺a, that annually brings together young adults and artists in a series of workshops that have continued to evolve. Since its inception, many hundreds of young people have engaged in the intensive young ev⁺a programme, culminating each year in an exhibition of artwork at the Belltable Arts Centre as a separate part of the overall ev⁺a exhibition.

The young ev⁺a project seeks to engage with young people as artists, providing them with the facility to broaden their perspective of the environment in which they live, to facilitate self-expression and understanding of their surroundings, and

to give a sense of contemporary art through creative activity. The project introduces young people to and involves them directly with professional art practice, allowing them to use contemporary art as a means of communicating and expressing thoughts, feelings and perceptions.

young ev⁺a participants, 2004 – David Bussoli, Conor Carmody, Bridie Casey, Lisa Casey, Mary Casey, Margaret Casey, William Coady, Marie Connors, Tess Connors, Vanessa Crawford, Joelene Egan, Nicole Galvin, Anne-Marie Hartnett, Michelle Hartnette, Jade Hehir, Lyndsey Keane, Jodie Keogh, Jeanette McNamara, Kelly Moloney, Mary-Ann Monaghan, John O'Donoghue, Maryann O'Driscoll, Shane Waters, Mellissa Whelan.

Group co-ordinators – Jackie Dwane, St Mary's Youth Project; Antoinette McLoughlin, Southside Youth Initiative; Margaret Casey, Limerick Travellers Development Group.

young ev+a 2004
Belltable Arts Centre, Limerick, 12 March – 2 April

ARTIST'S STATEMENT

These young teenagers have a story to tell, about themselves and their generation. The creative output of these young women reveals a contemporary idea of what it means for this generation to grow up in Ireland. The group, for me, forms a microcosm of the array of relationships that make up this city. I've discovered within these young women an innate desire to make images, stamping their mark on the world. Identity has become a key vehicle for the creative output of our workshops. Young ev⁺a allows young people to contribute to and participate in this city's cultural activity, rather than being mere consumers of it, creating a sense of familiarity and ownership of Limerick's art spaces.

— GILLIAN KENNY
young ev⁺a artist working with Southside Youth Initiative

Southside Youth Initiative
To identify and offer support to young people with a view to preventing their involvement in anti-social behaviour by providing positive opportunities for young people from the parishes of Our Lady of Lourdes, Queen of Peace, and the Holy Family. This will be achieved through a partnership with the community, voluntary organisations, and other relevant agencies.

ARTIST'S STATEMENT

After initially making preparatory images and recordings relating to the activities surrounding area and pastimes, we chose pool/snooker as our starting point to make further work. We played pool, photographed it, drew it, recorded it, and in the process explored a broad range of artistic languages and media. It was through the combination of these media that we developed the work for the young ev⁺a exhibition. Some of the work we made during the process chronicled specific events that took place. Other work transforms these events simultaneously into both histories and aspirations. Overall we explored the social event of the game, its mechanics, its widely varying rules, and, I think, how enjoyable it is to play. The lads made excellent work throughout the project, and created artwork we can all be proud of.

— MICHAEL McLOUGHLIN
young ev⁺a artist co-ordinator working with the St Mary's Youth Project

St Mary's Youth Project
St Mary's Youth Project works with small groups of young people in their own community, involving them in a range of activities and group work programmes. The project offers support to the young people in all areas of their lives, and strives to ensure family involvement.

Photographs of young ev⁺a participants on pages 171, 173, 175 by Maurice Gunning

ARTIST'S STATEMENT

I approached this project with a series of activities and discussions on make-up, fashion, dressing-up, performance, photography, video, and a trip to Bunratty Castle. The project focuses on a celebration of the group's culture and themselves, culminating in a series of photographic shoots exploring the rich and unique culture, femininity and identity of these young girls. Working with a photographic artist who employs the use of performance, the girls discovered a way to become directly engaged in a series of photographic artworks by using their physical selves. For the young ev⁺a exhibition we presented a series of photographs that displays their involvement in popular culture by their highly developed awareness of fashion, and also their sense of unity and strength as a cultural group as they pose and gaze assertively at the camera.

— AMY O'RIORDAN
young ev⁺a artist working with Limerick Travellers Development Group

Limerick Travellers Development Group
> To work towards a partnership of Travellers and members of the majority population, based on a respect for Travellers' culture, with the aim of promoting Travellers' rights, dignity and equality.

points of disorder in the rvm

An assessment of the artworks in ev⁺a 2004 will confirm once again the importance of the trend in contemporary art practice – increasingly favoured by artists and audiences alike – for the following:

1   the kind of literal-visual representation that stresses the narrative, the anecdotal, and the storyline with a reliance on the linear, sequential, and connected organisation of detail, and

2   the use of lens-screen-based media and the elements of design, integrated, and put at the service of literal-visual representation, and of the emotions and feelings that that kind of representation can refer to, arouse or express.

These kinds of stories can be told in all sorts of ways: through the media of film and digital photography, and video/DVD; through adaptations of recording/editing and graphic-design techniques (often with sound and image combined); and directly through written texts. (ev⁺a 2004 offers abundant examples of such storytelling.) Yet the artists working in these ways would usually prefer not to be considered as photographers or graphic designers or writers – specialists as such. Rather, they regard themselves simply as artists, who, in order to realise and express their ideas and concepts, remain open and flexible in their use of the tools and techniques of photography, graphic design, etc, and, for that matter, those of painting and drawing as well. Many contemporary artists when asked why, in the research and planning of their work, they choose to use photography or video over drawing or painting, simply say that the former are 'quicker'. The latter do take up far more time unnecessarily when the basic aim is, as it is in these cases, the acquisition of the look of things in the world at large, in images that incorporate the details of literal-visual representation.

This flexible approach to media-use means that there is no longer, in contemporary art, a hierarchical rating of media, just as there is no longer such a rating for subject matters; no subject or medium in today's understanding enjoys an inherent value advantage over any other. This levelling out of importance in the case of the work of art itself extends to the artists themselves. The concepts an artist is devoted to and their physical manifestation in the artworks do not exist only/or mainly to flatter or promote an individual artist's ego-name and reputation. Much contemporary artwork now comes to exist only through teamwork of one kind or another. This can happen within the identity of a specific group when the artists work together (sometimes almost anonymously); at times it is plainly acknowledged by name, in partnership with another artist; most often it occurs with the indispensable (and sometimes the extensive and complex) technical and aesthetic expertise of others. In these ways artists willingly share the responsibility for the artwork's existence, for its creative and technical presence before the audience. The artist will, though, maintain the identity of the initiator, the one who conceives and sets the idea or concept in motion, and remains in overall control of the process.

These instances of close collaboration on the part of artists, curators and technicians have a counterpart in the roles these artworks make available to their audiences. The images these artworks offer, the references they point to, centre on people and what people do. They deal with elements and events, issues and matters of concern that can be found in popular culture, matters that affect the popular mind; matters that are accompanied by a full array of political, social, economic and aesthetic contexts. To further the desired collaboration, these artists remain aware of and try to avoid the pitfalls of elitist positions as they strive to establish and maintain lively relationships with people in the world at large.

The commitment on the part of these artists to such subject-matters, and the way they are presented through lens-screen-based media, makes a great deal of sense, since our world – this urban, consumer world, and the people who inhabit it (ourselves) – are already deeply conditioned to similar combinations of representation, media, and design that we meet through the pervasive contact we have with what the entertainment and advertising industries offer us. Contemporary artists go to great lengths to ensure that their audiences can recognise themselves, or some part of themselves, and their world in the ideas and concepts the artists offer, and in how their offers are presented. When successful, such an aim encourages further collaborative effort on the part of the audience to co-make the meaning of the artwork. Often the works of art are designed and offered to the audiences less like commodities, and more like services. Attempts are made to escape the restrictions of the elitist fine art world of the gallery/museum by placing work in the hurly burly, humdrum world of alternative, off-site venues, in the contexts of shops, offices, churches, footpaths and streets. But other work, for all its intent to establish clear and intimate relations with the world at large, still requires a gallery environment. Its rigorous conceptual character, the relevant contexts it calls upon, and its reliance on lens-screen-based media (the dominant media of the world at large), with some irony, gains added advantage by meeting its audience within the exclusivity of the fine art gallery – a placement that is often the expressed wish of the artists themselves.

The emotions and feelings represented, aroused or expressed by works of contemporary art are also closely in step with the emotional life of the audience at large, with the feelings and moods that flood the urban/consumer world at large. This comes as no surprise since the ideas and concepts, the relevant contexts and the media preferences of these works are so deeply committed to participation in the life those people lead in that world. There seems very little outright joy expressed in these works, and little sense of praise given; rather, more of blame recounted. There does seem to be widespread feelings of anxiety over one matter or another; a sense of loss, of grievance, persists without the expectation of eventual redress.

But there is also a steadfast sense of confidence in the best contemporary artworks. This comes, perhaps, from the assurance these artists have that their work truly deals with matters real, with the real world, and the real people in it. This faith is rooted in the individual artist's ability to assess and pass judgement on her or his own existence in the world at large in relation to the encounters made with people at large; an existence that is far from ideal and one bereft of any ideals that promise real alternatives.

Some contemporary art, in response to this situation, provides the audience with spectacle, with impressive, self-important work, made on a grand scale (no matter what its actual size may be), in an attempt to come to terms with, to master, the anxiety, even if only on a partial or temporary basis. Other contemporary work, modest in such ambition, remains to an extent self-effacing, even humble, making little or no self-serving claim to a high or special position or to permanency; content to have its say and then quietly withdraw from any prominence. (For such artists, especially, documentation by a catalogue offers consolation and compensation.) Most contemporary art, whatever else it does, in whatever direction it chooses to take, involves itself, one way or another, in a common concern: its relationship to the rear-view-mirror presence of works of art of the past. There is always something in a work of art that refers to what it is as a work of art, and how it has come to be what it is in relation to the works of art that preceded it. For many, if not most, contemporary artists this concern centres on the works of Modernism, the example set in the works made by artists of the 20th century. Modernism, in all its variety of movements and styles, altered how representation (both literal-visual and emotional representation) and presentation (what a work of art actually, physically presents to the audience) interrelated in the way works of art were made. Literal-visual references lost their dominant role in representation, and the work of art's material, medium and design behaviour, what it actually presents, became as important, or even, at times, more important, in determining what a work of art had to say about itself and about people and the world at large.

These changes offered a challenge to the visual bias, a bias that lies deeply entrenched in the perceptual, intellectual and institutional life of the west. This bias maintains that sight is the pre-eminent sense in our perceptual life – a mistaken assumption first brought into prominence in Greek thought. It persists today even though we now have, through psychology, a far more accurate understanding of the structure and function of sense perception. Yet this bias continues to influence thought and feeling in ordinary, everyday experience, and, when institutionalised, in the directions taken and the advancements achieved by philosophical, scientific and technological investigation.

The radical Modernist changes affected the ways western culture expressed itself in works of art and extended itself in new technologies. But the basic institutional structures of the culture (and the assumptions about perception and knowledge at their base), firmly lodged in the systems of education, business, and government, did not change.

Slowly, but surely, at a cost of widespread confusion and suffering, Modernism's innovations have been subsumed to support some of the basic drives that have, for centuries now, led the west into global dominance. These drives can be recognised under all sorts of cover: The Belief in Reason; The Rise of Science; The Rule of Rationality; The Renaissance / Reconnaissance; The Reformation / Counter-Reformation; The Enlightenment; The Rise of Democracy-Capitalist / Communist; The Building of Empire; Manifest Destiny; Positivism; Faith in Progress; Utopianism; Secularism; The Command of Technology; Wars / Revolutions; The Shoa; The Rise of Consumerism; The Reign of Entertainment; Terrorism. Modernism, along with the radical changes it introduced in how best to make a work of art, became itself, in various ways, a cover for the ideas of Progress, Technology, Utopianism, Consumerism and Entertainment, ideas which have been called into question and often rejected by many contemporary artists and audiences. Rejection of the ideas has often meant, as well, rejection of those practical innovations that Modernism brought to the making of works of art, innovations that were the first successful challenges given to the rule of the visual bias. The teaching and training of artists, now in the hands of institutions of higher learning (as is the education of their audiences), has also meant that the value of those Modernist innovations that affect how representation and presentation function in a work of art, has been diminished. Today such institutions continue as havens and breeding grounds for the visual bias.

Contemporary art springs from how people (considered as artists and audiences – everyone is both) perceive and from the sense they make of the lives they lead, from the ways they express their thoughts and feelings as they discover and assert their identities as persons. Doing so means, in part, making proper use of the rear-view mirror by accurately assessing our present positions from correctly drawn references to the past. Since the artworks in ev⁺a 2004 have come from all directions, and, as such, truly represent international contemporary art as never before in ev⁺a, they provide and optimum opportunity for such an assessment.

PAUL M O'REILLY
Moycarkey, April 2004

exhibition of visual⁺ art – the ev⁺a story

The ev⁺a story begins in 1977 with artists based in Limerick who sought to bring their work into close collaborative encounters with audiences so that sense and meaning might be made of the world we all share. Nearly three decades on, ev⁺a, still an artist-centered exhibition, has become Ireland's premier annual exhibition of contemporary art. It now offers a wide-ranging programme of events that integrate local, national and international communities in the celebration of contemporary art and culture.

OPEN EV⁺A – the original approach – is an annual open submission exhibition in which all artists are encouraged to enter work in all materials, media, practices and styles. Each year, since 1979, an internationally experienced curator, an 'outsider' unfamiliar with the Irish art scene, single-handedly assesses the submissions (typically 500 works of art), selects the exhibition, decides on the character and layout of the exhibition in the galleries and alternative venues in Limerick city, determines the awards, and contributes a statement, essay and conceptual character to the ev⁺a catalogue.

YOUNG EV⁺A – a programme specifically for young people – was started in 1986 in conjunction with ev⁺a, and annually brings together young adults and artists in a series of workshops whose character continues to evolve. This has included a range of approaches – outreach with schools, engagement with community groups, and as a series of workshops in the gallery, and an Artist in the Gallery programme. This year young ev⁺a has focused on artists working with young people in the community.

INVITED EV⁺A – a special section begun in 1994 – is a biennial event in which the Open ev⁺a adjudicator of the year personally invites the participation of artists of international status, curates and places their work in Limerick city and its environs, thus providing a counterpart to the Open ev⁺a section.

THE EV⁺A COLLOQUIES ON CONTEMPORARY ART AND CULTURE – begun in 1997 as a biennial event – alternates with Invited ev⁺a. It consists of a weekend programme of informal sessions of discussion and argument among returning past ev⁺a adjudicators, invited guests, artists and audiences devoted to the ongoing attempt to make sense and meaning out of how contemporary art and culture interact and engage us in dialogue.

ev⁺a curators/adjudicators

1977 Barrie Cooke, John Kelly, Brian King

1978 Adrian Hall, Charles Harper,
      Theo McNab, Cóilín Murray

1979 Sandy Nairne (England)

1980 Brian O'Doherty (USA)

1981 Pierre Restany (France)

1982 Liesbeth Brandt Corstius (Neths)

1983 Invited Exhibition:
      recent work of past prizewinners

1984 Peter Fuller (England)

1985 Rudi Fuchs (Netherlands)

1986 Nabuo Nakamura (Japan)

1987 Ida Panicelli (Italy)

1988 Florent Bex (Belgium)
      Alexander Roshin (USSR)

1989 Invited Exhibition: recent work
      of prizewinners 1984-1988

1990 Saskia Bos (Netherlands)

1991 Germano Celant (Italy)

1992 Lars Nittve (Sweden)

1993 Gloria Muore (Spain)

1994 Jan Hoet (Belgium)

1995 Maria de Corral (Spain)

1996 Guy Tortosa (France)

1997 Invited Exhibition:
      Cross / Foley / O'Connell

ev⁺a colloquies on contemporary art and culture

1998 Paul M O'Reilly (Ireland)

1999 Jeanne Greenberg Rohatyn (USA)

2000 Rosa Martínez (Spain)

2001 Salah M Hassan (Sudan / USA)

ev⁺a colloquies on contemporary art and culture

2002 Apinan Poshyananda (Thailand)

2003 Virginia Pérez-Ratton (Costa Rica)

2004 Zdenka Badovinac (Slovenia)

ev⁺a awards

OPEN AWARDS

1990   Dorothy Cross,
Pádraig McCann
AFN Manson

1991   Robert Carver
(1754-91) and all 23
exhibitors equally

1992   Dorothy Cross
Shane Cullen
Kate Malone

1993   Liadin Cooke
Helen Comerford
Gavin Hogg
Brian Kennedy
Mick O'Kelly

1994   Felim Egan
Eithne Jordan
Kevin Kelly
Sharon Kelly
Gary Phelan
/ Mark McLoughlin
/ Brendan Bourke

1995   Michael Canning
Jeanette Doyle
Sarah Durcan
Cliona Harmey
Ronnie Hughes
Aisling O'Beirn
Amelia Stein
/ Nuala Ní Dhomhnaill
/ Cindy Cummings

1996   Mark Orange
Caroline McCarthy
Paul O'Neill
Rachel Toomey

1998   all 108 exhibitors
equally

1999   Sarah Durcan
Mary Kelly
Abigail O'Brien
Susan MacWilliam
Fergus Martin
Sandra Meehan
Mark Orange

2000   Maria Doyle

Caroline McCarthy
Deirdre Morgan
Ruth Rogers

2001   Ann Marie Curran
Susan MacWilliam
David O'Mara
Brian Walsh

2002   Amanda Coogan
David Dunne
Niamh McCann
Ciarán O'Doherty

2003   Christine Mackey
Jesse Jones
/ Joe Lee
/ Julie Merriman

PATRONS' AWARDS

1979   Felim Egan
1980   Tom Fitzgerald
1981   Tom Fitzgerald
1982   Breda Kennedy
1984   Jim Manley
1985   Tracy MacKenna
1986   Michael Creaney
Mary FitzGerald
Ann O'Regan
1987   Rory Donaldson
Richard Gorman
Finbar Kelly
1988   Eamon Colman
Tom Fitzgerald
TJ Maher
Peter Power

PAINTING AWARDS

1977   Graham Gingles
Alan Robb
1978   Anthony O'Carroll
Siobán Piercy
1979   Michael Coleman
Barrie Cooke
1980   Michael Coleman
Jack Donovan
1981   Ben Stack

1982   Anne Carisle
1984   Camille Souter
1985   Martin Yelverton

SCULPTURE AWARDS

1977   Robert McDonald
Eilís O'Connell
1978   David Leverett
James Buckley
1979   Roy Johnston
1980   Mike Fitzpatrick
Deborah Brown
1981   Danny McCarthy
Joanna Tracey
1982   Simon Moller
1985   Eilís O'Connell

GRAPHICS AWARDS

1977   Alan Green
Paul Mosse
1978   Joel Fisher
Brenda Keliher
1979   John Aiken
Joseph Lee
1980   Michael O'Neill
Don Mac Gabhann
1981   Donald Teskey
Miriam Flanagan
1982   Willie Heron
1984   David Lilburn
1985   Triona Ford

HONORABLE MENTIONS
(at discretion of adjudicator)

1977   Patrick Harris
Daniel O'Gorman
Benedict Tutty
Ian Sutherland
Michael O'Neill

ev⁺a publications

Since 1996, the annual ev⁺a exhibition has been documented in a substantial catalogue, with a keynote essay by the curator/adjudicator, and comprehensive documentation of all of the artists and works in that year's exhibition.

In 2000, a new, more book-like octavo format was adopted, with an illustration-led design. Each volume carries typically over 200 colour illustrations. This radical redesign has established the annual ev⁺a publication as the most visually arresting catalogue of contemporary art in Ireland.

The ev⁺a books are designed and produced by Gandon Editions. They are available from ev⁺a and through good bookshops nationwide, or direct from Gandon Editions.

ev⁺a 2003
on the border of each other

curator: Virginia Pérez-Ratton (Costa Rica)

featuring the work of 65 artists and a keynote essay, 'Landing in Limerick'

> "My wish has been to create significant clusters of meaning, that is, groups of works that relate one to another, and establish aesthetic, sensitive or conceptual links between them."
> — Virginia Pérez-Ratton

ISBN 0948037 032   24 x 17 cm   224 pp
268 col illus   €20 pb

ev⁺a 2002 – heroes + holies

curator: Apinan Poshyananda (Thailand)

featuring the work of 70 artists and a keynote essay, 'Concerning Heroes + Martyrs'

> "ev⁺a 2002 is a huge show ... it is also, though, more than usually accessible in terms of the intelligibility of the work. This may well have to do with Poshyananda's concentration on lens-based art ... As ever with art, the question of what the audience takes away from the transaction remains, but certainly ev⁺a deserves an audience."
> — Aidan Dunne, IRISH TIMES

> "Shows take place in venues around the city ... Art becomes part of the community instead of being something for 'other people' as sometimes perceived."
> — Marianne Hartigan, SUNDAY TRIBUNE

> "Featuring the exuberant and colourful work of 65 artists who manipulated visual images in galleries, shops, and public spaces all over Limerick, using every imaginable medium and discipline (and some indisciplines)."
> — BOOKS IRELAND

ISBN 0946846 871   24 x 17 cm   208 pp
223 illus (incl 209 col)   €20 pb

ev⁺a 2003 artists

Brooke Alfaro
Moisés Barrios
Milton Becerra
David Bourke
Kate Byrne
Susan Joy
  Connolly
Jennifer
  Cunningham
Dorothy Ann Daly
John Paul Dowling
  / Clare Gilmour
  / Ernest Bishop
  / Simeon Babo
  Tresor
  / Annette Young
  / Babatunde
  Longe
Joyce Duffy
Clodagh Emoe
Des Farrell
Larissa Fassler
Brian Flynn
John Gerrard
Claire Hogan

Deirdre Idema
Jesse Jones
Andrew Kenny
Gillian Kenny
Nicholas Keogh /
  Paddy Bloomer
Helen Killane
Gabriella Kiss
Marie-Josephe
  Lahaye
Luci Lane
Kerry Ann Lapping
Joe Lee
Seán Lynch
Eline McGeorge
Mark McGreevy
Margo McNulty
Susan MacWilliam
Christine Mackey
Sally Maidment
Lisa Malone
Nadia Mendoza
  Aguilar
Julie Merriman
Linda Molenaar
Priscilla Monge
Peter Morgan

Theresa Nanigian
Caoimhghín
  Ó Fraithile
Eamon O'Kane
Niamh O'Malley
Suzannah O'Reilly
Amy O'Riordan
Melanie O'Rourke
Raúl Ortega Ayala
Nadín Ospina
Derek O'Sullivan
Cecilia Paredes
  Polack
Caroline Patten
Liliana Porter
Una Quigley
Noreen Ramsay
Catherine Rannou
Christopher Reid
Joan Smith
Rafael-Ottón Solís
Beatrice Stewart
Gladys Triana
Massimo Uberti
João Pedro Vale
Orla Whelan

ev⁺a 2002 artists

Marina Abramovic
Nobuyoshi Araki
David Bourke
Kate Byrne
John Campion
Paolo Canevari
Gabriella Carlsson
Chandrasekaran
Ian Charlesworth
Martial Cherrier
Tim Coe
Amanda Coogan
Iftikhar and
  Elizabeth Dadi
Heri Dono
Andrew Duggan
Brian Duggan
Dunhill & O'Brien
David Dunne
Brendan Earley
Neva Elliott
Des Farrell
Tom Fitzgerald

Cai Guo-Qiang
Martin Healy
Sarah Iremonger
Mella Jaarsma
Choi Jeong Hwa
Peter Johansson
Garreth Joyce
Ömer Ali Kazma
Pauline Keena
Aileen Kelly
Anthony-Noël Kelly
Sarah Kenny
Maria Kheirkhah
Helen Killane
Arno Kramer
Prapon Joe
  Kumjim
Bernie Laherty
Karin Ludmann
Breda Lynch
Breda Lynch
Niamh McCann
Philip McCrum
Susan MacWilliam
John Mathews

Meredith Monk
Peter Morgan
Clive Murphy
Collette Nolan
Ciarán O'Doherty
Eamon O'Kane
Vanessa O'Reilly
Amy O'Riordan
Yvonne O'Sullivan
Ouch!Electro
Kamol Phaosavasdi
Áine Phillips
Deirdre A Power
Araya Rasdjarm-
  rearnsook
Heli Rekula
Torbjørn Rødland
Ronan Sharkey
Michael
  Shawanasai
Vasan Sitthiket
Catherine Slockett
Bernard Smyth
Lin Tianmiao

ev⁺a 2001 – expanded

curator: Salah M Hassan (Sudan / USA)
featuring the work of 90 artists, a keynote essay by
Hassan, 'Beyond Angela's Ashes', and an essay by
Medb Ruane

> "Salah Hassan, an enormously energetic
> presence on the international art scene,
> emerges from his Irish experience as an
> enthusiastic advocate of ev⁺a. It is, he
> reckons, a better model than the Venice
> Biennale: 'Venice is restrictive and
> outmoded. ev⁺a is more flexible and that
> makes it more forward-looking.'
>   Irish society has problems with the
> notion of multi-culturism, but, Hassan points
> out, 'Ireland *is* multi-cultural and multi-ethnic
> in terms of the various layers of its history.'
> It is an area, he suggests, that may yet
> fruitfully engage Irish artists."
> — Aidan Dunne, IRISH TIMES

ISBN 0946846 12X   24 x 17 cm   288 pp   374 illus
(incl 269 col)   €20 pb

ev⁺a 2001 artists

	Fiona Ginnell	Janet Mullarney
	Nina Grieg	Ann Mulrooney
Jananne Al-Ani	Stephen Gunning	Aisling O'Beirn
David Bourke	Victoria Hall	/ Marjetica
Ursula Burke	Karen Land	Potrc
Kate Byrne	Hansen	Treasa O'Brien
Michael Canning	Pat Harris	John O'Connell
Jota Castro	Catherine Harty	Alice O'Donoghue
Jota Castro	Lucy Hill	Augustine
/ Carmela	Katie Holten	O'Donoghue
Uranga	Noreen T Hopkins	Mairead O'hEocha
Ian Charlesworth	Allan Hughes	Eamon O'Kane
Jack Clarke	Tim Humphries	David O'Mara
Karen T Colbert	Emma Louise	Vanessa O'Reilly
Anthony Collins	Johnston	Amy O'Riordan
Phil Collins	Finola Jones	Alice Peillon
Oliver Comerford	Ruth Jones	Johannes Phokela
Jean Conroy	Catherine Kelly	Catherine Rannou
Ann Marie Curran	Gillian Kenny	Willie Redmond
Patricia Curran	Helen Killane	Ben Reilly
Mulligan	Aidan Linehan	Peter Richards
Alan Daly	Niamh McCann	Gina Ryan
Dorothy Ann Daly	Eoin McCarthy	Cóilín Rush
Angela Darby	Ronan McCrea	Peter Savage
Joyce Duffy	Eline McGeorge	Zineb Sedira
Rita Duffy	Julie McGowan	Dan Shipsides
Andrew Duggan	Dara McGrath	Joan Smith
David Dunne	Eoghan McTigue	Camila Sposati
Clodagh Emoe	Susan MacWilliam	Anne Slocket
Carissa Farrell	Christine Mackey	Tracy Staunton
Des Farrell	Caroline	Sue Townsin
Barry Fitzpatrick	Masterson	Denise Walker
John Gerard	Madeleine Moore	Brian Walsh

ev⁺a 2000
friends + neighbours

curator: Rosa Martínez (Spain)
featuring the work of 39 artists and a keynote
essay, 'The whole ev⁺a experience'

> "As ever, ev⁺a plunges the viewer into a
> raging battle between art and life as artists
> go forth to site their work amidst the
> chaotic indifference of Limerick city centre
> ... an illuminating and provocative presence
> in the city..."
> — Sarah Durcan, CIRCA

> "Almost everything tests and resets the
> onlooker's baseline of reality or normality.
> Colour and busyness abound on every page
> ... Invited curator Rosa Martínez' account of
> her experience is refreshingly untheoretical
> and exudes enjoyment."
> — BOOKS IRELAND

> "The EV⁺A catalogue is an example of
> Gandon's dedication to the contemporary art
> scene in Ireland."
> — WATERSTONE'S GUIDE TO IRISH BOOKS

ISBN 0946846 405   24 x 17 cm   192 pp   225 illus
(incl 179 col)   €20 pb

ev⁺a 2000 artists

	Katie Holten	Fidelma O'Neill
	Alan Keane	Ebru Özseçen
Ghada Amer	Bernie Laherty	Tadej Pogacar
Colin Andrews	Ernesto Leal	Deirdre A Power
Janine Antoni	Caroline McCarthy	Pipilotti Rist
Xu Bing	Edwina McDonagh	Ruth Rogers
Bernadette Cotter	Christine Mackey	Bülent Sangar
Alexandre da	Deirdre Morgan	James Savage
Cunha	Darren Murray	Anne Seagrave
Beth Derbyshire	Aydan	Santiago Sierra
Maria Doyle	Murtezaoglu	Bernard Smith
Federico Guzmán	Nikos Navridis	Seán Taylor
Mona Hatoum	Rivane Neuen-	Charlene Teters
Carl Michael von	schwander	Sergio Vega
Hausswolff	Veronica Nicholson	Gregor Zivic

an ev⁺a compendium

(invited ev⁺a exhibitions of 1994/96/98, and 1997
ev⁺a colloquies on contemporary art + culture)

editor: Paul M O'Reilly

> "The importance of this event is that it has
> brought new ideas from around the globe to
> Ireland, and introduced Irish artists to a
> wider international audience ... The
> Compendium offers a chance to assess the
> movements and ideas ... and the essays
> themselves are provocative."
> — Jane Humphries, BOOKS IRELAND

> "seeing an outsider's view of something with
> which you are familiar – that's part of the
> appeal of EV⁺A"
> — Marianne Hartigan, SUNDAY TRIBUNE

ISBN 0946846 278   23 x 23 cm   216 pages
125 illus (incl 110 col)   €15 pb

invited ev⁺a 1994
Steven Bachelder
Bizhan Bassiri
Marcel Biefer
   / Beat Zgraggen
Kathe Burkhart
Berlinde de
   Bruyckere
Luc Deleu
Fausto Delle
   Chiaie
Wim Delvoye
Jessica Diamond
Mike Fitzpatrick
Dan Graham
Ann Veronica
   Janssens
Mariuz Kruk
Bernd Lohaus
Rogelio LÓpez
   Cuenca
Bruce Nauman
Royden
   Rabinowitch
ManfreDu Schu

invited ev⁺a 1996
Alain Bernardini
Christian Boltanski
James Coleman
Dorothy Cross
Braco Dimitrijevic
Willie Doherty
Thierry Fontaine
Jakob Gautel /
   Jason
   KaraÎndros
Paul-Armand Gette

Felix Gonzalez-
   Torres
Paul Graham
Marie-Ange
   Guilleminot
Thomas
   Hirschhorn
Fabrice Hybert
Valérie Jouve
Ilya Kabakov
Brian King
Bertrand Lavier
Marie-Ange Leccia
Alistair MacLennan
Gilles Mahé
Alice Maher
Jean Luc MoulÈne
Tania Mouraud
Marylène Negro
Walter Niedermayr
Maurice O'Connell
Martin Parr
Gary Phelan
   / Mark
   McLoughlin
Kathy Prendergast
Nigel Rolfe
Uri Tzaig
Lawrence Weiner

invited ev⁺a 1998
Cecilia Aaro
John Aiken
Martin Assig4
Chung Eun Mo
Michael Coleman
Franky Deconnick
Rineke Dijkstra

Marlene Dumas
Maurizio Eletrico
Peter Fischli
   / David Weiss
Karin Giusti
Richard Gorman
Rodney Graham
Karl Grimes
Thomas Grünfeld
Andreas Gursky
Tjibbe
   Hooghiemstra
Johnathan
   Horowitz
Robert Janz
Johannes Kahrs
Mike Kelley
Ciarán Lennon
Zoe Leonard
Stephen McKenna
Janet Mullarney
Jorge Pardo
Richard Powell
Joe Scanlan
Seán Shanahan
Ben Schonzeit
Mariella Simoni
Amelia Stein
Johan Tahon
Michael Timpson
Luc Tuymans
Juan Uslé
Jan Van Imschoot
Walter Verling
Michael Warren
Daphne Wright

ev⁺a 1999 – reduced

curator: Jeanne Greenberg Rohatyn (USA)
featuring the work of 62 artists and a keynote
essay 'In many ways, we were strangers...'

> "Greenberg eschewed risk and worked hard
> to bring together a show that behaved itself.
> Rather than an artists' brawl in the Cedar
> Tavern, she gave us a party in a beautifully
> renovated SoHo loft, where half the guests
> were in recovery and the rest were baking
> their own bread."
> — Peter Murray, IRISH ARTS REVIEW

ISBN 0946846 26X   23 x 23 cm   164 pp   94 illus
(incl 89 col)   €15 pb

ev⁺a 1998 – circus zz

curator: Paul M O'Reilly
featuring the work of 108 artists and a keynote
essay 'ev⁺a 1998 – a report'

> "Apart from its sheer size, the huge and
> hugely ambitious show infiltrated the city so
> well that it was sometimes indistinguishable."
> — Aidan Dunne, IRISH TIMES

ISBN 0946846 189   23 x 25 cm   168 pp   117 illus
(incl 114 col)   €15 pb

These books can be ordered from ev⁺a, through any good
bookshop, or direct from Gandon Editions (same-day
dispatch; postage free in Ireland, worldwide at cost).

send me   ____ EV⁺A 2004 – imagine limerick   €20
          ____ EV⁺A 2003 – on the border...   €20
          ____ EV⁺A 2002 – heroes + holies   €20
          ____ EV⁺A 2001 – expanded   €20
          ____ EV⁺A 2000 – friends + neighbours   €20
          ____ an EV⁺A compendium   €15
          ____ EV⁺A 1999 – reduced   €15
          ____ EV⁺A 1998 – circus zz   €15

❑ payment enclosed by cheque € / stg £ / US $ _____

❑ charge to Laser / Mastercard / Visa a/c   [MasterCard] [VISA]

   # __ __ __ __ __ __ __ __

   __ __ __ __ __ __ __ __

   exp __ __ / __ __   security code __ __ __

name _____
                              PRINT NAME & ADDRESS
address _____

_____

GANDON EDITIONS Oysterhaven, Kinsale, Co Cork
t +353 (0)21 4770830 / f 4770755 / e gandon@eircom.net

artists' index

Carlos Amorales MEXICO / NETHERLANDS * 15, 20-23, 167, 168

Julieta Aranda MEXICO / USA * 15, 156-157

Yuri Avvakumov RUSSIA * 15, 24-27, 162, 167

Maja Bajevic BOSNIA * 15, 28-31, 170

Sarah Browne IRELAND 15, 32-35, 170

Dieter Buchhart AUSTRIA 15, 36-37, 167, 171

Gerard Byrne IRELAND* 10, 15, 38-41, 166, 167

Ben Cain UK 15, 42-45, 163, 167

Mircea Cantor ROMANIA / FRANCE * 1546-49, 165, 167

Phil Collins UK * cover, 2-3, 15, 50-53, 167, 168

Mark Cullen IRELAND 15, 54-44, 166, 167

Ann Curran IRELAND 15, 56-59, 164, 167

Alexandre da Cunha BRAZIL 15, 60-61, 162, 167

Janine Davidson IRELAND 15, 62-65, 168

Brian Duggan IRELAND 15, 54-44, 166, 167

Ayse Erkmen TURKEY * 15, 66-67, 169

Vadim Fishkin RUSSIA / SLOVENIA * 15, 68-71, 161, 165, 167

Tina Gverovic CROATIA 15, 42-45, 163, 167

Leonora Hennessy IRELAND 15, 72-73, 168

IRWIN SLOVENIA * 15, 74-77, 161, 169

Emily Jacir PALESTINE * 15, 78-81, 164, 167

Emilia & Ilya Kabakov RUSSIA / USA * 15, 82-85, 164, 167

Johanna Kandl AUSTRIA * 1586-87, 166, 167

Ziga Kariz SLOVENIA * 15, 88-91, 161, 163, 167

Gillian Kenny YOUNG EV*A 173, 174-175

Alyona Kirtsova RUSSIA * 15, 24-27, 162, 167

Michael Klien AUSTRIA 15, 92-93

Volkmar Klien AUSTRIA 15, 94-97

Borut Korosec SLOVENIA 15, 98-101, 161, 170

Ed Lear UK 15, 94-97

Paul McAree UK 15, 102-103, 170

Eline McGeorge NORWAY 15, 104-107, 169

Michael McLoughlin YOUNG EV*A 173, 176-177

Christine Mackey IRELAND 15, 108-109, 170

Katrina Maguire IRELAND 15, 110-111, 163, 167

Dusan Mandi SLOVENIA * 74-77, 161

Dorit Margreiter AUSTRIA * 15, 112-115, 164, 167

Maxine Mason UK 15, 116-117, 166, 167

Miran Mohar SLOVENIA * 74-77, 161

Aisling O'Beirn IRELAND 15, 118-121, 167

Roman Ondak SLOVAKIA * 15, 122-123, 162, 167

Vanessa O'Reilly IRELAND 15, 124-125, 171

Amy O'Riordan YOUNG EV*A 172, 173, 178-179

Alan Phelan IRELAND 15, 126-127, 162-171, 167

Anri Sala ALBANIA / FRANCE * 15, 18-19, 128-131, 163, 167

Andrej Savski SLOVENIA * 74-77, 161

Efrat Shvily ISRAEL * 15, 132-133, 167, 171

Nedko, Veselina & Dimitar Solakov BULGARIA * 15, 134-137, 164, 167

Malin Ståhl SWEDEN 15, 138-141, 167

Mladen Stilinovic CROATIA * 15, 142-143, 169

Apolonija Sustersic SLOVENIA * 15, 144-145, 161, 167, 168

Fiona Tan INDONESIA / NETHERLANDS * 15, 146-149, 165, 167

Sally Timmons IRELAND 15, 150-151, 167, 171

Roman Uranjek SLOVENIA * 74-77, 161

Aleksandra Vajd SLOVENIA 15, 152-155, 161, 165, 167

Anton Vidokle RUSSIA / USA * 15, 156-157

Borut Vogelnik SLOVENIA * 74-77, 161

* = INVITED ARTIST